WORDS
from a
WIDE
LAND

WORDS

from a

WIDE

LAND

William D. Barney

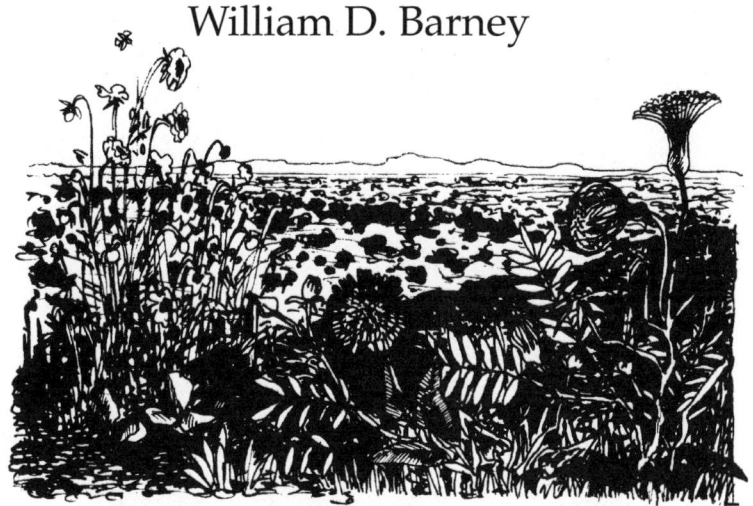

University of North Texas Press

Printed in the United States of America

10 9 8 7 6 5 4 3 2 1

Permissions:
University of North Texas Press
Post Office Box 13856
Denton, Texas 76203-3856

This book is printed on recycled, acid free paper.

The paper used in this book meets the minimum requirements of the
American National Standard for Permanence of Paper for Printed
Library materials, Z39.48.1984.

Library of Congress Cataloging-in-Publication Data

Barney, William D., 1916—
Words from a wide land / by William D. Barney.
p.   cm.
ISBN 0-929398-64-5
1. Barney, William D., 1916—   —Diaries. 2. Poets,
American—20th Century—Diaries. 3. Poets, American—Texas—
Diaries. 4. Natural history—Texas. I. Title.
PS3503.A61855Z475   1994
818' .5403—dc20
[B]   93-29508
CIP

Jacket Design and Illustrations
by Caissa Douwes

ACKNOWLEDGMENTS

Some of the original notes from which certain of these entries came provided material for poems published in *The Killdeer Crying* (Prickly Pear Press), *Descant, A Galaxy of Verse, The Pawn Review, Voices, Wwhimsy, Hyperion* (Thorp Springs Press), *A Texas Christmas* (Pressworks Publishing, Inc.), and in other books by the author: *Permitted Proof* (Kaleideograph Press), *Long Gone to Texas* (Nortex Press), *In a State of Euphorbia* (Bullnettle Books) and *Listening Back* (Counterpoint Publishing Co.).

FOREWORD

Anyone reading this book may wonder how it came to be written, and from what sources entries were taken.

Early on I fell into the habit of writing notes about what I saw or heard, or read, or thought. I did not think of this as a journal or a diary. Rather, as "observations." My thirty-five years in the Postal Service in various capacities took me to many corners of the country. Our family traveled when we could. Many things caught my eye, odd ideas popped into my head, and I liked to make notes. The same urge was true of home life, or of hours commuting between Fort Worth and Dallas, and of days spent at the Fort Worth Nature Center and Refuge. I set down notes when I could find time. To me, this seems a way of holding on to whatever gives a peculiar zest to existence.

Authors who have written pages for every day of the year appeal to me. The present book is no almanac, though some entries are seasonal. Neither are the years in consecutive order. I trust I may be borne with if from time to time I have departed from standard prose. Such patches break up a stolid look to the page. A little bit of everything is in the pot.

Certain entries provided material for later poems. I found these notes a rich source, sometimes turning one of them into a poem many years after the actual occurrence. Even so, the notes have had a unique power to stir my memory.

I wish to speak my warmest thanks to my friend, Tom Dodge, whose resourcefulness led directly to finding the publisher of this book.

—William D. Barney

JANUARY

JANUARY 1

1936— In the oil field: Daily the hot tamale vendor pushes his cart by the warehouse. The sky is an eerie backdrop from the light of gas flares as he cries at the top of his voice, "R-e-d H-o-t!" followed by a little rainbow of song, "Ha-ah-ah-ah-hot!" (do-mi-sol-mi-do). Then he completes his call with "Get 'em hot A-L-L the time!" Whereupon my brother Fred in the warehouse office repeats the whole aria back to him.

JANUARY 2

1968— Downtown: Looking up through skyscrapers, their tops shrouded in fog. In such a manner do the insects look through the grass and see only a small way up the stalks? Or man, looking up through one Galaxy, see only the shins of the Universe?

JANUARY 3

1975— The same people who transformed the watch
      into a luxury of great price and beauty
      are at work on the common calendar.
      I cannot find in a store twelve pages of dates
      to which some frill of art or whimsy
      is not attached. All I ask of a calendar

is, tell me what day it is.
Art I welcome in its place, but spare me
hybrids. In years past
I have seen calendars that made me forget
not only the day but my age. Even they are gone.
Of certain low persons I've heard it said
they'd not give you the time of day.
What point in history have we come to
when men no longer give you the time of year?

JANUARY 4

1955— Every night now we chase the day westward from
Dallas to Fort Worth, from late afternoon through sundown,
afterglow, to darkness. As fast as the bus may go, the day is
fleeter. Where a while ago I saw particulars, now I see only
masses. The last tinge of saffron has been washed from the
sky. We are like creatures fleeing a prison: the spotlight that
was on us for an instant has passed beyond.

JANUARY 5

1971— On a sleepless night the realization comes
 I cannot rest in any symmetrical position.
 There has to be some overlapping of bones,

odd angles here and there,
as if to protest the daylight stiffness.
I see now that the limbs of the dead
are hardly arranged for their own comfort
but only to fit the coffin's dimensions.

JANUARY 6

1975— Today saw a roadrunner on Scenic Drive. I suspect
him of being our Chaparral in Residence, and not just some
visiting Lizardist.

JANUARY 7

1957— In the establishment of city delivery at De Leon I
came to interview Mrs. W. E. Lowe, whose letter to President Eisenhower prompted action by the Post Office Department. She had long worked to see such service provided, she
had an eightieth birthday approaching, and it would make a
nice birthday present.

She proved to be a fascinating woman. She came to De
Leon as a "trimmer," a window dresser. Originally a teacher,
she had no intention of working in stores, but a friend per-
suaded her to go to Dallas where a merchants' convention
was in progress. A man needing a trimmer began to work on

her to go to De Leon (her home was near Baird). She finally consented to go, told him she would double his money for the first year or not take the job. First thing off she charged twenty-five dollars for a hat and sold it, despite his unbelief.

She was quite a belle, but always told men they had to go home at 10 P.M. She would take down the clock if they did not. Various swains pursued her, but she became interested in Widower Lowe. She even talked around that she was going to marry him. He too became interested and came to see her shortly before Christmas; she told him he could come but she would have to wrap Christmas packages. "He is no better than anybody else," she informed a friend, "even though I am going to marry him someday." He stayed past 10 P.M. and neither of them noticed until the eleven o'clock whistle blew. When he got back to his boarding house, envious men were sitting around waiting an explanation how he did it. When she went home for Christmas, they all made her promise to write and she did send them postcards. But to Mr. Lowe, when they all went together for their mail, a letter was waiting. Later, when they were married, during the First World War, she went with him to a bond-selling campaign in an area that was "Bolshevik." It had been rumored anybody trying to sell bonds would get shot. The meeting proceeded, with every-

one reluctant to mention bonds. Finally, she did the job herself, and even convinced some hard-bitten farmers to come to Mr. Lowe's bank and buy bonds.

She tangled with an election judge who was not putting ballots in the ballot box. Went to Comanche, the county seat, and got the thing straightened out. She tore her own ballot up and people thought she had done worse than rob a bank. One woman told her there wasn't anything worse than that. Mrs. Lowe told her she was the most ignorant woman she had ever seen and walked out. She also told two brothel owners she would give them three days to move their bawdy house, which they had set up near the edge of town. They moved overnight. She also attacked the mayor over repair of a ditch in front of her home.

She once told Postmaster Tate Counts that the post office was the poorest-run place in town, that the clerks had no manners, and that she held him responsible for it. Eventually, we made her a bit happier with the postal service. With the help of George Ross, an old hand at postmanship, city delivery was established in a matter of days. The very first letter was delivered by a postal official riding up to her door on the back of a fire truck. The letter was from President

Eisenhower, a birthday congratulation, for this was the very day, her eightieth. And I had the pleasure of singing "Happy Birthday" to her.

JANUARY 8

1969— A little shift in the angle of sunlight
gives us the sunrise and the sunset;
a little tilt in the Earth's axis makes the seasons turn.
Blessed be obliquity,
without which nothing beautiful comes.

JANUARY 9

1982— A cold but sunny day to plant some fruit trees. This called for a supply of water, and I took the hose I had drained and connected it to the back hydrant. At first, nothing came out, and finally, only a feeble piddle. I inspected the hydrant—the water was on, I could hear it. I checked the hose for kinks—there were none. Then I noticed the flow was increasing. The fitting had come off the end before it was stored, and now I noticed something protruding from that end—an icicle. I pulled it out, and promptly, another took its place. This process followed for several minutes. Delightful!

It was like a sow giving birth to a litter of pigs. I went into the house to call Mary to see something wonderful. But too late. All I had to show were a few icicles.

JANUARY 10

1972— On the morning walk I tried to reason out the spacing of icicles, why on horizontal limbs they should hang so uniformly, the same distance apart, the same length of body. Is there some complex relationship between surface tension, gravity, and freezing that makes for this strange orderliness? I can perceive that in an ordinary rain the drops might run until their accumulated weight pulled them from the undersides of limbs. But how can they freeze in such intervals?

JANUARY 11

1980— In exchange for books of mine that they sold on consignment, I bargained with the Nature Center for twelve sacks of buffalo chips, collected by the Explorer Troop to finance an expedition to Big Bend. It seemed a fair trade, because I needed fertilizer for my garden and didn't mind the price. Something might be said about whether the buffalo made as much of a contribution to this Earth as I had with my book, but let that pass. It was my first experience with this medium

of fertility. I was told most of the chips were reasonably new, but that was not always true. Many were hardened to a concretelike consistency; I couldn't shatter them with a blow of the shovel but had to chop them apart with the edge. An odd thing about them: some insect had tunneled through the older clods, leaving a reddish corridor. That puzzled me, for I know of no red clay near the surface in the buffalo pasture. It remains to be seen how the soil of my garden responds.

JANUARY 12
1956— The black street repairmen this bitter cold morning warm their feet by turning the blowtorch, with which they are working in hot asphalt, on the soles of their shoes.

JANUARY 13
1978— After the ice storm of two days ago
    the sun is out bright, and I hear
    the sound of dripping everywhere.
    The trees this morning are chandeliers.
    From a pile of leaves in the garden
    an intermittent cloud of vapor arises,
    almost as if someone were under the stack
    exhaling, puffing out white breath
    as frail as my own.

JANUARY 14

1971— After a freezing night, from a high point overlooking the lake, we saw a great blue heron standing on the ice off Greer Island. From time to time he would fly, then alight, skidding or skiing a little as he did. It looked pretty certain to us that he was enjoying the experience.

JANUARY 15

1977— At times, reading a book,
>   I discover I'm doing no such thing
>   but have drifted off the margin.
>   In Life too I sometimes suddenly see
>   I haven't been really living at all—
>   just turning pages.

JANUARY 16

1981— The whitecaps off Idlewild. At first I thought them ice floes but as we dropped lower I could see the white dissolve and disappear. We observed a wreck involving four policemen and three women pedestrians in Times Square, this as we went toward the Hotel Astor. The ambassador from Syria, Abou Omar Riche, sat at my right and was most courteous. At his right was Richard Wilbur, civil, quiet. A con-

trast to Theodore Roethke, who was drunken, offensive, profane. "What are you, a God-damned Baptist?" he asked (I wasn't sporting a drink). Robert Frost, slightly bent, growing frail, but his mind still very sharp. He quipped that Frank Dobie had probably put me up to it—receiving from his hand the $1,000 check for the Robert Frost Memorial Award.

JANUARY 17

1978— Here is one of those great Unexplained Mysteries that profoundly demonstrate how some things simply do not admit of explanation: the way in which my shoestrings become uneven in length, no matter that at intervals I patiently weave them back through their eyelets to parity. Maybe this is a parable of riches, which regardless how often divided, soon distribute themselves back to the Haves while the Havenots look on and dwindle.

JANUARY 18

1975— The sparrows dustbathe where my peas
     have just broken through the ground;
     I doubt they will bother the plants
     though they make little craters throughout the rows.
     Anyway, sparrows are lousy little birds.

They need all the help they can get
halfway through winter.

JANUARY 19

1976— Digging in the garden after a winter rain
I came on a horde of earthworms nibbling on leaves
I'd buried. Where do they come from in such
   numbers?
They must have the skill of swifts and swallows
such as men used to think spent winter
in the mud of lake bottoms.
Or they have some way of skewering down
deep into earth till they get to where
it begins to stay hot—
and then, one day—a sniff of Spring?

JANUARY 20

1961— The starlings did not know what to make of the In-
augural Parade, which lasted until long after nightfall. In the
window from which I watched on the fifth floor of the Post
Office Department building, a dead starling lay crouched in
a corner, the sill thick with their excrement. Its imbricated
feathers blew softly as it lay oblivious.

JANUARY 21

1969— In the woods, every once in a while,
I see the blasted trunk of a tree, bare of bark,
disclosing a body ruinously twisted.
Not in one part only, but throughout,
so that I wonder if the roots too are tortuous.
Why a tree grows thus in a forest
of a thousand of normal grain, I don't know.
Maybe like a man
with an extra chromosome. I know nothing
in the life of a tree that would justify
calling it a sinner.

JANUARY 22

1978— Our second snow within the week.
This quiet Sunday morning everything is white-still.
The twigs across our driveway
exhibit a strange prickliness
of little crystals of ice or snow—
as if incoming flakes had struck edgewise
and stuck at right angles to the stem.
Some of the leaves appear
as spiny as holly.

JANUARY 23

1982— I walked the railroad from North Side Drive to its intersection (overpass) with I-35. Found it no easy task to walk, either, because the roadbed ballast consisted of egg-sized chunks of granite. I tried walking between the rails; two ties are too short, and three ties too long a stride. I could not walk easily away from the ties because the granite offered no comfortable footing. The best walking was on the ties outside the rails. As a boy I walked many a railroad and never had any such difficulty. Such is progress.

JANUARY 24

1981— I don't understand, in the first place,
        why or how there should be a Me
        who should attempt to understand.
        Secondly, I don't understand why or how
        there should be Space, infinite or otherwise,
        for something to take place in.
        Thirdly, that Matter should be what takes place.
        Fourth, that at least a part of Matter
        appears to have been organized
        or organized itself—I do not understand at all
        how this came about without

some kind of direction. Most of all,
I don't understand how there could be
a How if there is no Why.

JANUARY 25

1966— We watched the coming of the snow under the streetlights, great swarms of strange insects pouring noiselessly down upon the earth. Their motion was such that some appeared to have tails 1ike comets, and we debated whether this was an illusion. Which I think it was, but Mary said no, they were real. I will remember our walks in the snow, those muted torrents of half-light, half-shadow, and most of all the warmth and illumination of the one beside me.

JANUARY 26

1972—No doubt of it, I am losing the ability to hear the higher   notes of birds, for Mary calls my attention to passing cedar waxwings I do not detect. My eardrums are thickening or growing brittle. But no use to bewail. I shall be putting more and more of myself in pawn as the years and days come on. Why not do it with as much grace as I can muster? I see nothing to be served by raging against the going.

JANUARY 27

1975— The warmest day on record at eighty-one degrees. At evening I looked out the back door and saw a frenzy of small moths dancing over the driveway, wild as children let out of school.

JANUARY 28

1975— The elm trees, like a certain kind of woman,
                shown the least bit of warmth
                want to put out flowers
                almost in the middle of winter.

JANUARY 29

1982— Went with the grandchildren to the great annual event of the Stock Show Parade. Rain threatened, so we went prepared. We stood in the middle of Houston Street on the north side of Weatherford, where the parade turned south; just as the parade began, at 2 P.M., drops of rain began to come down in earnest, but they let up and gave no further problem. This was odd: A young man came up to me just before the first drops and said, "There is going to be one of the damnedest exoduses you ever saw. There is a humongous storm about to come in." His information was dead wrong.

Some new features in the parade. A man riding a Brahma steer. A wagon with four white German police dogs. A man in enormous boots and enormous cowboy hat playing the part of a western gunfighter: he stood about seven or eight feet high in those boots. A huge Brahma transported on a hay-filled wagon. One of the delights of the parade is the playing of predominantly black bands: this time there were two or three such, and by the time the parade had made its circle to Sixth Street, over to Main, and back to the court-house and west again on Weatherford, each band had been joined by a long tail of cheering young blacks. The air, as the streets became damp from the spit of rain and as the innu-merable horses passed, began to reek of horse manure.

The crowd was not quiet. Some hawkster selling long blue-colored horns had passed through, and a good many youngsters were blowing them, making noises not unlike the bellows of cows. There were Clydesdales, in tandem, but we missed the huge horses of the Budweiser wagon. A harness of them, not so dark brown as those of Budweiser, did appear at the end of the parade, pulling a steam calliope—such as I've never seen before in the parade. It advertised the Fandangle at Fort Griffin and gave off vast clouds of steam as it played; someone said you could hear it thirty miles away.

I can't imagine how the lady playing the thing could hear
what she played. And last of all, my favorites, the gaggle of
street sweepers, mechanical giants doing their duty efficiently
but not being able to rid the pavement entirely of a yellow
stain.

JANUARY 30

1972— What moves the starling outside in my yard
to imitate a bobwhite? A poor job he does,
and there he goes aping a killdeer.
It seems he struggles to be articulate,
that he hates commonness, longs to be
some blither bird.
I'm afraid he's a poet.

JANUARY 31

1976— The other day I ground horseradish
out of curiosity—to see could I make sauce.
Clumps I planted yielded great leaves
but hardly a nodule underground.

I had to await the appearance
of roots in the supermarket.
Still, grinding them, I was brought to tears—
to think, at last to achieve
successful sauce!
A small thing in a mechanistic world,
but my own.

FEBRUARY

FEBRUARY 1

1948— The most exciting event of the entire Fat Stock Show!—the unloading of a truckful of hogs. It took four men, prodding and pushing and pulling ears with all their might. All this to the hellbrew of squealing that drowned out even the cursing, all done to get the hogs to the end of the truckbed and out on the gangplank. Once their front feet were on the plank, they would look about with a sort of offended hauteur and amble more or less nonchalantly down. But until this could be accomplished, they burrowed into the front corners of the truckbed as if in holy fear of the outside world. One of them shot violently between the legs of the fellow who pulled on its ears.

FEBRUARY 2

1970— I never observe without wonder
      the marvelous helmsmanship of a bird
      coming in at full speed, braking himself,
      dodging limbs and arriving at a perch
      with such exactitude of timing as to appear
      a certainty. And it is certainty,
      a miracle repeated a billion times a day.
      The speed of calculation,

the weighing all factors of flight,
obstruction, distance—the solution achieved
with such ease it seems almost contemptuous—
enough to bewilder the eye of a man.
It is not only the sparrow's fall
that is worthy of mark, but his alighting.

FEBRUARY 3

1961— On the Washington streets I saw a demented fellow who imagined himself to be dressing a company of soldiers. He studied imaginary lines and constantly cursed them to "dress it up." Several times, however, he waved a little silly wave at somebody who didn't exist and would run a few tip-toe steps. Then he would revert to bowing and squatting and straw-bossing his company of soldiers.

FEBRUARY 4

1976— Before the garage door, in the lee of its shelter from the north wind, I noticed a cluster of doodlebug craters. What are they doing here in the dead of winter? Obviously, a few warm days have brought the small ants abroad (them I did not notice), and no sooner did they journey forth than those who prey on them set up their booths.

FEBRUARY 5

1953— Looking back on the trip to New York City to receive a share of Borestone Mountain prize: New Yorkers know how far into the dark they go. Nearing Grand Central you ride into the darkness for an interminable length, and then all about you people suddenly know it is time to rise. I could discern nothing.

FEBRUARY 6

1977— My mind at night—a tiger prowling
        back and forth in its cage? Not at all.
        More like a bee, crawling over a hive,
        tasting one cell after another
        and steering through honey without regard
        for what is contiguous.

FEBRUARY 7

1968— This morning as I stepped out on the front porch, a strong south wind was blowing, and I smelled cedar—straight off the juniper-covered hills of Somervell and Johnson Counties, a good thirty miles away.

FEBRUARY 8

1970— Went with the Joe Loweses to Paluxy country, to
Rock Church, a beautiful old two-story rock structure. The
first floor still had a few pews of the church that once met
there. Another part was used for a school. The upper story
housed a Masonic lodge. The walls were desecrated with the
sentimentality of adolescent scribbling. Over and over someone had written in large letters, "I love you, Carolyn." Below
the church is a suspension bridge over the Paluxy; to the north
the cemetery with many old tombstones.

FEBRUARY 9

1976— Today while I planted broccoli
    a cabbage butterfly paid me a visit—
    or rather the young plants I was setting out.
    She flitted ecstatically around one plant
    I had put in the ground, and then could not resist
    even the one I held in my hands.
    What had she done (I could almost hear
    her words) to deserve such bounty?
    Well, she was the first of her kind
    out on a sunny day in February.
    She deserved to be rewarded.

FEBRUARY 10

1978— At the Robert Burns dinner I watched Annie Strathdee served a wedge of pie, it being set before her with the point away. A curiosity struck me, and I nudged my neighbor to watch also. "What are you saying about me?" asked Annie, suspiciously. Conducting a psychology experiment, I explained. Sure enough, before she began to eat, she first turned the point of the pie toward her. All along the table this was true. There seems to be no necessity for this—you can eat as well from the ear of a piece of pie as from the nose. Still, people (myself included) will turn the point of the pie toward them like an indicator before they snip the first bite.

FEBRUARY 11

1975—The ragged little line of robins
          that chased the winter north a week ago
          has fallen back in disarray before the resurging cold.
          Or are these rather the last reserves,
          the elite guard, thrown into a still raging battle?

FEBRUARY 12

1966— As I came home on a foggy morning following a cold night, I could see turkey vultures working very hard to get

and stay aloft. Or maybe they were flying low to look for breakfast under the fog.

FEBRUARY 13

1951— In the hospital they let me listen by stethoscope to the near-to-arriving baby's heartbeat. A little tom-tom or gas engine. Outside in the hall, a sort of Stock Exchange chart posted the progress of deliveries. Perspiring, chalk-faced mothers wheeled by us down the hall to the recovery room, a dark tomb of pain and near-unconsciousness. Nurses unmasked to announce, "You have a boy, Mr. X" or "a girl, Mr. Y." What a thing to announce: a birth, a beginning.

FEBRUARY 14

1978— As we came home from church in the rain, there on a power line over the river sat a red-tailed hawk, about his business of death. In such wretched cold weather I couldn't help feeling a bit sorry for him, for he has to survive somehow. If it weren't for some equally wretched rodent that thinks it has to survive, the hawk wouldn't stand a chance. At the end of the day he was still perched there, cold, hungry (I have no doubt), but still deadly in his patience.

FEBRUARY 15

1971— We went for a drive to Palo Pinto country and along the Brazos. Many cardinals in the festoons of grapevine alongside the river; scaup upstream. Two farm wives stopped their pickup trucks in the middle of the ford to gossip. At Palo Pinto Lake, the overlook pleased us. As did the outcrops of stone, heavily scabbed and stained with lichen.

FEBRUARY 16

1972— The buds of the cottonwood begin to sharpen,
      the cardinal is repeating himself,
      forsythia is in bloom.
      There will be no holding back the signs of spring.
      I will play a game with myself to see
      how many markers of its coming I can recognize.
      The pace will quicken: soon they'll be coming
      faster than I can greet them.
      I will be drowned in the flood of arrival.

FEBRUARY 17

1959— The porter on the Texas and Pacific at was telling the people to move up to the other car for Little Rock con-

nections. "What you got in heah, yo' cookstove?" he asked one black woman as he assisted her with bags. There was great giggling as he carried on his banter among several black women. "Yo' set right there and enjoy yo' coffee, and then when yo' gets through yo' gonna have to put yo' shoes on and move to the next car." In front of me sat a staring-eyed woman who seemed almost drunken from her talk; at the least, there was an unsteadiness and slowness in her speech. "Here comes a fella sellin' stuff," she said, without feeling of any kind, though I gathered she was hungry. Later, I heard her deploring the near-alcoholic state of some women she had just visited.

FEBRUARY 18

1972— Those sleek, immaculate creatures,
      the cedar waxwings—who would have thought
      their toilet habits so abominably messy?
      Their droppings are not droppings, they are spurtings;
      that diet of mistletoe and holly
      gives them a wide palette with which to spatter,
      and the world's their canvas. Still,
      who can resist them? We love our infant children
      and they are soilers too.

FEBRUARY 19

1978—After the night's heavy snow we went out for a walk, and suddenly we were conscious of a great quietness over the earth. The freeways were still, no planes in the sky, no vehicles moving on the streets. I could not help thinking: how wonderful it must have been to have lived in the days before all these marvelous inventions came to make noise.

FEBRUARY 20

1981— As I filled my tank at the gas station a youth of about fifteen came wheeling up to the air hose on a low-slung bicycle. I heard the tire pop when he put too much air into it, and then I heard an oath and a crash—he had flung the bicycle about twenty feet out on the side street. He went to it and threw it another twenty feet, and when I last saw him he had it hoisted over his shoulder and was walking off in disgust to the inevitable repairs.

FEBRUARY 21

1970— That old analogy—
       finding the perfect watch—
       will not in this age establish
       a Watchmaker. I prefer the picture

of a germ, a virus, suddenly become aware
it is launched in the vessels
of an unimaginable Brain.
And all about, a seethe and flow
of incredibly complicated thought
and surpassing beauty are taking place.

FEBRUARY 22

1964— The temperature is a delightful seventy degrees. I
see the buds on the peach trees are swelling; a daffodil has
opened its yellow trumpet; narcissus, though hard-bitten by
the winter, has displayed its white stars. Henbit has unfurled
its small crimson tubes. On the lilac bush I detect tiny pebbled
bumps of purple pushing toward the day of bloom. The elm
is showing small leaves. A cardinal is singing. In the neighborhood a troop of blackbirds struggles in a crooked song.
Finally, on the redbud, little strawberries stick out along the
bare limbs. And into the cool soil I have planted radish seed,
kohlrabi, onion plants and bulbs, and six collards.

FEBRUARY 23

1978— Mary says she finds herself unconsciously awaiting
the arrival of the morning mail, and when it comes it seems a

weight falls off her shoulders. I don't know why. Not a day passes we do not receive solicitations from Indians, Republicans, Preservers of Whales, Democrats, Redwoods, or something else imperiled.

FEBRUARY 24

1975— Wayne Clark told me of efforts to transplant a colony of prairie dogs from their town out on the Poly Freeway to the Nature Center. They flushed the rodents out, using a thousand-gallon tank of water under pressure. This was augmented by a sudsing compound such as used in detergents—the combination always drove the dogs to the top, where they sat in great confusion, bubbles all over them. They could then be picked up with a capture-stick. But it had to be done quickly, for some were stubborn enough to dive back into the hole and drown. A portion of the Refuge was fenced off and holes were dug for them, which the dogs used as long as human beings were around. Nevertheless, they quickly deserted this retreat, and the hawks and a red fox or two soon caught on to their presence. Twice they have been resettled, twice exterminated. It remains to be seen if the transplant succeeds.

FEBRUARY 25

1983— North of Fredericksburg Mary and I decided to make the climb to Balanced Rock; we found it rugged indeed—she almost backed out but kept on climbing. The path, marked by painted white arrows, led through great boulders of granite, difficult footing. It occurred to us how foolish we were, for if one of us had fallen, broken a bone, the other could have been helpless. There were a few other, younger people making the climb, however. I was surprised to find so many colors and varieties of lichen on the granite: red, orange, yellow, green, black, gray, both pale and dark. Atop the steep hill the trees, many of them live oaks, were swaddled in ball moss; on some twigs I saw two varieties of lichen and ball moss, side by side. The geological patience of the lichen, slowly turning the mountain into boulders, then into crumbs, struck me, as well as the irony of it: here we subjected ourselves to all manner of disequilibrium in order to see a rock in equipoise. And when we finally came to the viewing place, some fool had painted his initials in large letters on the flank of the mighty boulder.

FEBRUARY 26

1976— When I dig up an earthworm
        by accident, depriving him of life,
        I have to reflect: I can do this
        only because I am bigger,
        presumably more intelligent.
        But his title to the land is all as good
        or better than mine—
        he has truly invested in it.

FEBRUARY 27

1955— Two men engaged in a hot quarrel on the courthouse steps this afternoon. One in overalls had a New Testament open, and the other, plainly angry (and with spaces between his teeth) was arguing vehemently. The argument apparently was going his way, for the man holding the testament seemed cowed.

FEBRUARY 28

1981— Now comes the first rain for what seems
        months or years.

I watch the circles instantly formed
on standing water—joyous loops quick with energy;
almost before I see, they have spread, collided
with other rings, and disappeared
in the general flux. A paradigm, I might think.
But this is no cause for melancholy:
the great thing here is not
the shortness of being, but the delight,
the vivacity, the ecstasy in it.

FEBRUARY 29

1976— I picked a cottonwood bud and found it gummy and
aromatic, just as the books say. I was surprised, however, to
find that the faint sweet odor stayed on my fingers even after
I had washed my hands.

MARCH

MARCH 1

1955— In the field yonder a farmer on a tractor is plowing with a disk plow. He circles his field, cutting off the margin somewhat in the way your mother used to pare an apple in one long peel. Or as you might unwrap a cinnamon roll. It is like working one's way into a maze instead of out.

MARCH 2

1959— There is something about the pungent smell of a skunk, encountered from the safety of a car and coming only for a short moment, as it will on our highways, that I can't help appreciating. It is vigorous, bracing; it has the quality of wildness and stings the sense more than any sight or touch or sound can equal. I am almost relieved to know that something is left that is not only not civilized—it is not even civil.

MARCH 3

1981— One of those blue-green-yellow days
    of Texas in March: the earth has put forth
    a fresh cover of grasses and forbs;
    the sky is washed clean by yesterday's rain; every
       where

lawns are generously sprinkled
with shining dandelions.

MARCH 4

1955— There in the middle of a post oak thicket
a half dozen wild plum trees bloom—
children in white dresses
lost in a still dead wood.

MARCH 5

1978— Who else will speak for me? said the Light.
Who else say what I have to say?
Of waddles upon green lily pads?
Of stinging hair of the bull-nettle
where I break through? The luster of musselshell,
the windows of the downtown bank
in October sunset? The shape of oak boughs
at six o'clock on a March morning?

MARCH 6

1962— After months of drouth, it begins to rain with the
abandon of someone too long deprived of love. As we leave

in the dark of morning, robins are drinking from the puddles in the street. Almost blinded by our lights, they barely escape being run over.

MARCH 7
1978— One thing we could always see about the moon was that it is round. Even when it isn't all there, the curve guides the eye in a full circle; we fill in what is missing. There is a piece of dark that doesn't count.

MARCH 8
1981— My walk took me down a railroad spur and under the overpass that carries Interstate 35. To explore such a place is like lifting a rock to examine the underworld: the difference between the hustle and hum of traffic above and the isolation and solitude below cannot be described, it must be felt. The explorer soon learns others have been before him: on the wide face of concrete abutments, adolescents have painted obscenities. Which do not exactly blush unseen, yet only an occasional engineer in the cab of a switch engine is likely to know the words exist. It leads me to think on the scope of graffiti under bridges, confined generally to four great subjects: Love, Religion, Politics, and Sex. Except for Money, these comprise the main interests of humanity.

MARCH 9

1972— It is hard to believe we are in the dangerous part of the year, when a sudden freeze is still possible. The other night a mockingbird woke me with his singing at 3 A.M. Redbud, plum, pear are in bloom, a host of lesser trees and shrubs. And still we have not reached the average date of the last killing frost.

MARCH 10

1972— The seasons are to us like the successive skins of a toad, which are cast off when they have outlived their usefulness. But the image is reversible: do not the summer, the winter, one day cast us off also, in order to emerge into a primer Time?

MARCH 11

1972— Try only to set down
       the commonplaces that are otherwise
       swallowed up by the hours. The redbud in the yard
       is in full bloom—had we not known it well last year
       and the year before, we would be wonderstruck
       by its loveliness today. How can I pass casually
       as I have done a dozen times this morning
       without saluting, raising a cheer?

I suppose if we could not grow dull
in the face of beauty, likewise, we could not learn
to tolerate pain and ugliness.

MARCH 12

1978— As I passed the new bank downtown, the wind battered the halyards of the flagpole in a steady rhythm, much like a Salvation Army lassie ringing her bell in Christmas season.

MARCH 13

1967— This morning moths hover in the jasmine bloom, dodging from flower to flower frantically and gorging with their curlewlike swills as if they fear a sudden freeze will cast down the whole crop.

MARCH 14

1992— I feel like a murderer because I am forced to protect my lawn from an infestation of fire ants. They have come unbidden, and if permitted to stay would proliferate and make the place untenable for human feet. I hesitated to use poison on them, as I do not want to poison the soil. I dug a hole in two mounds and poured boiling water into them. The sight of

so many, many little creatures who must suffer makes me think I have committed genocide.

MARCH 15

1958— Not-to-be-forgotten sound: The pop of the newspaper boy's bundle as in the dark before dawn he breaks the wire that bands his papers together.

MARCH 16

1981— Whitney State Park: A pleasant day, though it cooled rapidly as night fell. We placed the kitchenette outside the shelter, to have the warmth of the sun, and Mary fried chicken. As she took it into the shelter her grip on the frying pan slipped and the chicken landed on the concrete before the door. What would any reasonable person do? She washed it off and reheated it, and we enoyed it thoroughly, not minding a few pieces of grit. After dark I was reading *Tess of the D'Urbervilles* to her, when suddenly she shushed me: animals at the front of the shelter were fighting over the remnants of grease still on the concrete. I took the lantern and went to the screen door and shined it out. Instantly, I saw a flash of black and white disappearing. Almost as instantly, a wave of odor swept in. Fortunately, it was not long-lasting;

even more fortunately, I was not actually sprayed. It taught us a lesson: don't assume coons in skunk country.

MARCH 17

1978— The old rancher who drove a busload of children to the Nature Center remarked, after seeing the stuffed rattlesnake, that a rattler can strike in two different ways. One is the pose of the exhibit (you might call it "standard rattlesnake"); the other is the way of a snake that almost fanged him last fall. The weather was getting chilly and the snake did not rattle a warning. He came within eighteen inches of it before he saw the viper, and it was coiled with its head and neck raised in the shape of a question mark. In that position it can strike its fangs into flesh with the greatest force possible, really sink them deep.

MARCH 18

1982— As I looked out the window I could see Lori, the little girl next door, leaning far back in the seat of her swing and happily moving back and forth, dragging her beautiful long red hair in the dirt.

MARCH 19

1977— As I work in the garden
            a quiet little song—two beginning chirps
            and a long fluttering trill—
            comes from the post oaks. It is the same field
                sparrow
            I caught in binoculars a week ago
            in the pure art of melody—
            no mistaking who produced it.
            But what is a field sparrow doing
            in my city yard? Has he been here before,
            years past, and I mistook the song
            for some other bird's? Impertinent questions.
            All that matters is, he is blessed with voice
            and I with ears.

MARCH 20

1971— For seizing upon intuitions, tenuous perceptions, I
advocate using the mind much like a robin does its head. That
is to say, exercise a sidelong look at things that do not lend
themselves to being viewed squarely. There are elements and

activities of this life that exist only in the periphery of the conscious and may be caught only by an unfocused glance.

MARCH 21

1977— This morning I hear the chickadee
      singing the variations
      of his four-note lovesong.
      One is a simple, innocent little turn,
      the other the same tune
      with his resonating chamber on.

MARCH 22

1977— Our neighbor's English walnut has great thick catkins on it, the size of my little finger. The mesquites are beginning to leaf out—we can hope that spring has truly arrived. Bur clover is in yellow bloom in the lawn, the Mexican buckeye on Dalford Hill begins to flower just as the redbud is being swallowed up in its leaves. Hackberries are putting forth. The catkins on the Shumard oaks have turned brown and look almost like small clumps of Spanish moss.

MARCH 23

1976— In Tyler, where we went to see azaleas and dogwood in bloom, we saw some unfamiliar large oaks at one home with colorful plantings and asked the owner what they were. She didn't know but wished they were back in the swamp—look what they had done to her sidewalk. The roots weren't visible, but they had made a young sierra out of the cement. The leaves looked like those of a Durand oak, and digging around I found shiny, chestnut-colored acorns with a shallow cup—enough to cinch it.

MARCH 24

1975— We stopped in Pascagoula, Mississippi so that Mary could take a picture of a big ship loading. In order to get a picture we wound our way along an opposite side of a bay and found a place that purportedly sold seafood. But no, they were fixing up the place as headquarters for a shark-fishing venture, said the young lady. She was quite intelligent and gracious. She and her husband fish for shark at the mouth of the Mississippi by winter and off Key West in the summer.

They use a 1500 foot line with a thousand hooks, figure on getting a 10% catch. Each shark will measure eight to twelve feet long. They save the skin and the fins (for soup), but the rest is jettisoned.

MARCH 25

1981— In the garden I discovered a brand new if somewhat brutish pleasure: standing over the collards—which no amount of pruning will keep from bolting into buds and flowers—and biting off the green heads. A deerlike browsing, this, done without the aid of hands. And the mouthfuls taste clean and a little sweet.

MARCH 26

1967— There are special gauges of the passing of life that are a peculiar treasure to me. Catkin-time must be reckoned among them. The mulberry is pushing out small processes that look like little clubs. The cottonwood has dropped knobbed spikelets. The oak is pink with putting forth leaves as its catkins dangle.

MARCH 27

1975— We drove to Rip Van Winkle Gardens on Jefferson

Island, Louisiana. A pleasant surprise. In one place we saw a camphor tree. Much bamboo in a very lush setting. Some of the most beautiful live oak trees we had seen, including the "Cleveland Oak," under which Grover Cleveland siested when visiting. We drove on to Breaux Bridge: I hoped to find the little cafe by a bayou where I once ate crawfish. Sure enough, there it was, just south of the town. We dined on crawfish, Mary eating étouffée and I boiled crawfish. The waiter had to tell me how to do it. You crack the tail first, then peel off the shell after you pull the tail off. She also said to crack the head off and scoop up some of the fat if there was some to be seen. I tried this, but it didn't appeal much.

MARCH 28
1968— Light snow falling in West Texas. From the plane it appears to etch the contours of the earth—everywhere snow almost obliterates the lines. Where the fields are freshly plowed, the snow has melted, leaving rectangular plots standing out in a world of white.

MARCH 29
1968— There he is, his whitish breast shining as he sits on the top strand of a barbed-wire fence—the first scissortail of

spring. It means the sun has returned to our hemisphere, the insects have begun to stir, and this old nemesis is back to punish them.

MARCH 30

1955— A dust storm is thickening over the countryside now at 6 P.M. after a heavy downpour and hail. The groundlights are on at the airfield, and a plane comes rocking from wingtip to wingtip as it shoots into the air over us; it has disappeared into the gray murk before I can complete this sentence. The Texas fields have taken on the appearance of English moors, the distant woods look to be half-buried in what might be thought fog. The wind is out of the Panhandle, the breeder of these storms, and it is cold and spiteful. If I look upward at about a forty-five degree angle I seem to see the top of the dust cloud. Overhead, blue sky can almost be made out. You feel this damnable dust in your throat and you can perceive it in the ghostly manner in which it obscures the landscape. But for the most part it merely hangs and sifts and diminishes distance.

MARCH 31

1976— In Tyler State Park, the last week of March,
the fireflies are already at work
punctuating the night. Like coals
the winter could not extinguish,
they set the woods afire with spring.

APRIL

APRIL 1

1976— In two places on the trail of the Boardwalk at the Nature Center we saw tent caterpillars at work, or at least going through some activity akin to labor, agony, or the twitch. Those outside the web jerked and writhed constantly as if the stuff around them had been heated to a burning pitch. For that matter, those inside, seen murkily, also gyrated. Feeding? Growing pains?

APRIL 2

1944— In the hotel dining room at Granbury an old fellow bragged about his knowledge of the fiddle and fiddle-calls. He sniffed about the efforts of two girls from the Baptist Seminary who had rendered a duet. "What singin'?" he asked. "I didn't hear no singin'." Postmaster Chevis Cleveland pointed out a building where John Wilkes Booth is supposed to have lived a short while after supposedly escaping. He would, when a little too drunk, mount a barrel and spout Shakespeare. He and another man visited a saloon in Fort Worth and passed a soldier, who remarked, "If that ain't John Wilkes Booth I'm a liar." Shortly afterward, "Booth" disappeared and was never heard of again.

APRIL 3

1981— Today a great branch- and bough-weaving day,
the sky overcast, the wind coming in heaves.
Downtown I had to stand on the curb
with one foot planted in front of the other
for fear a gust would blow me into the traffic.
Never has wisteria been more passionately
    outpoured;
it is everywhere in long clappers of blue.
The photinia bushes are huge fountains of white.
Across the street under the mulberry trees
the pavement is covered with a thick swarm
of chartreuse caterpillars—
soft, fuzzy catkins fallen from the boughs.

APRIL 4

1977— All these high-sounding oracles,
pseudo-statements, delivered as if
from the throne of Reason, without a trace
of uncertainty—Life is not like that.
Life has all kinds of exponents,
modifiers, qualifying clauses, pluses
or minuses. It is like working your way

through a dense equation, patiently removing
the clutter, until at last you catch a glimmer
of what the real problem is.

APRIL 5

1975— Whenever the green collard makes up its mind
(or whatever's in its roots, since it doesn't yet
have a head) to go to seed, there's no stopping it.
I tried, one spring, lopping off flowers
as fast as they opened. But like true revolutionaries
not to be denied, they came back ever faster.
Meanwhile, the blades refused to grow broad
but put out only narrow straps.
The collard's time had come; it set its course
toward making fruit. There was no stopping it.

APRIL 6

1983— It has been two weeks since we had the old cottonwood cut down; it was an old friend, giving us both shade
and music, but it had become a menace, leaning over the
house with heavy limbs that the approach of spring winds
made perilous. Hardly a week after it came down a storm hit
our neighborhood that split oak trees. I gathered some loose

branches that had caught in the pecan trees and stacked them in the garden for later disposal. And now I notice that the buds have opened into leaf on the severed boughs; they persist in the hope of life even after the fatal cuts have been given.

APRIL 7

1977— Walking up Sylvania, I came across the keys of a maple tree fallen on the sidewalk, looking for all the world like cicada wings. I remember a huge maple in my boyhood, and when you squeezed these seeds between thumb and finger, they shot out a jet of green juice. No doubt of it, the world was juicier in those days.

APRIL 8

1976— As far as I know, nobody has celebrated
rightly, the way the twigs of the jujube grow—
a grievous oversight I make haste to amend.
What other tree matches this zigzaggery?
This looking left, then right, in a man
would mark the caution of a sea captain
in submarine waters.
What does the jujube fear? Nothing.

It only makes a pattern on air,
something of its own. Perhaps it needs to hold high
those great burly joints or, on the other hand,
maybe it delights in angles.
Whatever, I like the jujube's gesture.
It's not afraid of being itself.

APRIL 9

1955— No other structure tells as much history as a fence, particularly a barbed-wire fence. Even a short observation will disclose marks of struggle with fire, erosion, with heavy-footed animals and the two-footed who pry the strands apart for passage. You can read almost as you will of the habits and luck of the builder. I doubt you can tell his character. I myself would appreciate a good fence but probably build a poor one. It would do for my purpose if it stood up, but it would lack art. It would likely show that I don't care much about a straight line nor worry about a tinge of decrepitude in this or that. It might even show a certain amount of contempt for the idea of fences.

APRIL 10

1976— I grudgingly admire creatures

like warblers and haws, which have their own
    ways
of identifying themselves (mere onlookers
can't tell at a glance which they are).
Of course they infuriate me,
as men do who keep their own counsel and will
    not be read
by every Tom, Dick, and Harry.
These unique beings do have one disadvantage,
    though:
given a chance, men will dissect them
in order to discover their true character.

APRIL 11

1964— On Greer Island the first of oak leaves, pink to scarlet, beaded with mist. The fructification of lichen, small cups
lifted like grails if you looked closely; spider webs everywhere, made visible by the fine wetness. In an open space, a
dead copperhead. Someone had cut off its head. The bee tree
on the north with an orifice like female genitals; the sedgelike
plant with seed pods still hanging; a dragonfly clutching a
leaf, where it sought cover from the damp.

APRIL 12

1976— A scented communication
        from the garden.
        And bearing only a small signature:
        "Your umbel servant,"
                DILL

APRIL 13

1973— At about 4 A.M. I heard a mockingbird awake in the dark, singing ecstatically, as if he had had the opposite of a nightmare.

APRIL 14

1983— We found Paisano at last (some trouble because a street sign was turned), reaching it over an extremely rough road, rocky rather than gravelly. The gate to Frank Dobie's old place has a rusty figure of a paisano on it. It seemed miles from this gate to the ranch house; we crossed Barton Creek just before reaching the house. Russ and Ann Vliet greeted us warmly. He seemed as excited as I to have this first encounter in person. Heretofore we had had only a delightful exchange of letters.

He quickly told us he would prepare a cactus salad (it being near noon); he set about cutting young buds off prickly pear at the corner of the long porch. We scraped the thorns off the lobes, and these he boiled, producing a mucilaginous brew that, with tomato, proved quite tasty. Rice vermicelli, mushrooms, and other bits formed the main dish. We enjoyed listening to Ann and him thrash out the problems of the meal. She is a lovely companion for a poet-novelist, being forthright, practical, affectionate.

The interior of Paisano is, of course, filled with memorabilia of Dobie and Frank Wardlaw and others who have had a part in the history of the place. Paintings, photographs, artifacts abound. Ann had a new electronic typewriter, which she proudly showed us. Russ opened his study, where he writes in longhand. I recall he said he had always written with a penstaff, dipping in ink.

They have been married around thirty years, went somewhere to school together. She was reared in Gruene, outside New Braunfels. He spoke with feeling of having lived for a time south of Mexico City, where they found the people—true peasants, I suppose—most considerate and helpful. In Vermont they lived for twelve years in a rural place with no

electricity. When his illness developed, they saw that a change would have to be made, and they now want to buy a lot in San Marcos and build a small house.

We went, the four of us, for a walk up the hill behind the house, looking at red buckeye, an old stone fence, wildflowers, enjoying a varied conversation. And after that sat on the porch with more of the same. He showed me one of my own books in which he had written, in the margins, various comments. He always does this with books, he said.

We left reluctantly, over their protests, as evening came. It seemed to us that an instant bonding had formed, one of those rare friendships that burst into bloom happily, almost by chance.

(We were to see Russ only one more time, when he and Ann stayed with us overnight on their way back to New England. Much as I relished those long, yellow pages in his bold script, I did not write him, not wanting to place the burden of replying on him. A letter from Ann told us of his death in May 1984. Just about the time he finished his last novel, he suddenly began to lose strength, but finish it he did. He was a remarkable person. I miss him.)

APRIL 15

1981— At Ennis on the Bluebonnet Trails, and elsewhere when we stopped by a field and the wind enveloped us in their fragrance, it was like wallowing in the bed of an odalisque. Maybe that's why Mary had misgivings about their almost overpowering scent.

APRIL 16

1968— I see the aperture of my mind
          is not such as to seize truth
          in the least available light.
          It must have longer shutter speed, time
          for the image to sink in. Brains
          are no different than cameras; all get the same
               amount
          of light, but the couplings are different
          for iris and shutter. And so is what is seen.

APRIL 17

1967— At the head of Westbrook Street the mesquite is now in catkin—long yellow tassels of flower hang in the boughs, and beneath, on the street, the asphalt is covered with a yellow seedlike snow.

APRIL 18

1977— Part of the joy of gardening
is finding a place to grow something
you have no room for.

APRIL 19

1970— I am not satisfied with my life,
but I am pleased with my portion.
I was born this day in a great free place.
I was taught love of music, books, religion.
I found a lovely and faithful wife.
I have assisted at the birth of two sons
and waited for two others. I have seen many
strange and exciting scenes, and have dealt
in contentment at home. Grief and pain
came to me, though not in such measure I
could not bear them.
In not many years death shall escort me out of
this circle.
I have not tasted all the honey
nor all the gall; notwithstanding,
my cup has generously brimmed.
I am glad for my time upon earth.

APRIL 20

1972— The Lincoln sparrow comes as the rarest;
        shy, unobtrusive, handsome but not showy.
        You have to look for him if you hope to see him.
        And yet, on occasion he is overcome
        with the beatitude of existence and breaks forth
        in a quiet song of triumph.
        In the commonplace din of the city
        it is like being suddenly presented
        midway in a roaring organ passage
        with a delicate air on the harpsichord.

APRIL 21

1952— Downtown, the lion-head (mountain lion or panther, actually) carvings along the cornices of the Flatiron Building, each holds a mouthful of grass and string. Sparrows' nests. In truth, the Lion Shall Eat Straw.

APRIL 22

1955— Something I like about bluebonnets (and Lord spare me any more paintings) is their upstandingness. They run in a soldierly file up and down the roadside in full uniform and with complete military dignity. The Indian paintbrush is not

so: it is more relaxed and more individual. Likewise, the pink evening primroses, which arrive like wild children wherever they will to appear.

APRIL 23
1972— We took the footpath to Boquillas Canyon despite the growing heat. As we topped a ridge we saw a Mexican sitting on the opposite of the Rio Grande, a burro nearby. As we proceeded, he mounted his burro and began crossing the river at an angle plainly intended to intercept us. He seemed harmless enough, and when he finally came to shore just as we reached the same point on the trail, he smiled: "You wanna buy some rocks?" In his extended hand he presented some bluish crystals.

APRIL 24
1949— To plant okra seed in the furrow
    as the first great drops of an April shower
    begin to pelt the soft soil—
    to firm the soil hastily, and then run
    as the downpour begins in earnest!

APRIL 25

1970— A transformer is knocked out.
We sit in our house
without light save for a few candles.
And now we learn this: electricity
is piped into houses to light up inhabitants,
to make them incandesce and move.
When did I lie in utter relaxation, thinking as I
    pleased—
no book, no lamp, no keeping time with clocks?

APRIL 26

1978— Forty-nine years ago in the spring after my family
came to Fort Worth to settle in Oakhurst, I found the beard-
tongue and the evening primrose called the fluttermill spring-
ing up on the limestone bluffs that look down on our little
trickle of a river. Today I went bicycling, and there they are
again, blooming in profusion as madly as the vast choir we
heard last night singing Verdi's *Requiem*. I am content. If
fifty years can pass and make little difference in what chooses
to live and exult on this patch of hill, then I have hope to
keep my own voice raised a few years longer.

APRIL 27

1960— Northwest the lightning pulsates at one point and then another as though the hand of a skillful cellist reached with deliberately quavering fingers here and there on the throat of the storm to give it vibrato. Or it flickers in the same way the skin of a sensitive mare shudders to dislodge a cloud of flies. Not only to the ear but to the eye a coming thunderstorm has multiple rhythms.

APRIL 28

1980— We drove to Lake Whitney, Buchanan Dam, Echanted Rock, Gorman Falls, hoping to see many wildflowers; and we did see them, but not in the profusion we had expected, probably because of the dry, mild spring. We walked out on top of Buchanan Dam to the sluice gates and observed hundreds of cliff swallows building or tending nests. We could not see the nests from our position above the birds, because they built under a small overhang that concealed them from us. This is strange country, with vast outcrops of granite here and there, some in great conical piles, some in sills, much of it spotted with lichen. At Enchanted Rock southwest of Llano I noted seams or cracks that ran in the

huge dome for many feet in a straight line. Entering the park we ran over or passed over a long snake, light-colored, very possibly a rattlesnake, which writhed into the grass.

APRIL 29
1976— On a windy day the pennons of a used car lot sigh and sing like a pine forest before an approaching storm. I imagine a boy from a country town hearing them and becoming lonesome for the piney woods of East Texas.

APRIL 30
1978— Had I never seen an iris bloom
        could I believe the report
        from some more fortunate corner?
        Yet here they are in my yard,
        a dozen different shades and pastels,
        delicate, virginal tissue,
        each singing its own magnificat
        whilst I putter around with a water can.

MAY

MAY 1

1970— Someone, I see, has loved even a mesquite tree enough to tend its wound with tar. Yet others tell me you cannot be too solicitous for this rough native's health. Water it a touch too much, it will die.

MAY 2

1956— On the hills around our city the first spikes of yucca are appearing, creamy and callow—perhaps with a touch of green in their texture, as best I can see from here, which cannot yet be called white.

MAY 3

1977— I plucked a bit of shepherd's purse that I found growing on the sidewalk—and with the touch of the leaf to my tongue I was carried back to my childhood. Such is the magic carpet of the taste buds.

MAY 4

1978— With half my plunder from a reading
I bought two magnificent volumes,
Ricketts's *Wildflowers of Texas*.
It's as though I had to expiate

for the sin of poeticizing
by some gesture of extravagance.
But never mind: nothing will bring me greater
    delight
than getting to know the prairies of Texas
which in this month of May
are wild with excitement.

MAY 5

1938— Magnolia bloom in full display this week, four or five to the tree, each bloom held up, a glistening silver goblet or a resplendent grail toasting its maker. The scent of some is sealed almost completely within the unopened bud: with the unfolding a swooning drowsiness permeates the air.

MAY 6

1980— Something ought to be said for the pleasure of not being rained on; that I live in a house with a good porch where a body can take a dry seat and watch the drops coming down is no minor comfort. There is no false feeling here that a person ought, for some obscure moral reason, plunge into the wet to face the torrent and the cold. Nothing of that sort of guilt a man might feel on becoming aware of less fortunate

men. No, a solid roof overhead and a porch deep enough that the rain does not blow in on him will give any man a sense of the fitness of good cover, of the reasonableness of sound structure, of the sheer enjoyment of being snug in the neighborhood of the elements.

MAY 7
1966— Mary and I watched from our bedroom window upstairs a pair of cedar waxwings in the red mulberry tree playing the game of Pass-the-Mulberry. Back and forth, they must have exchanged it twenty or more times. What is this, an Alphonse and Gaston act? No, it isn't too much to ask of my supposedly superior intelligence to imagine that these birds are enjoying themselves.

MAY 8
1975— At the Mayfest the lady demonstrating the spinning wheel said it is difficult to card wool in Fort Worth because the water is hard. Members of the spinning guild catch rainwater to wash their wool in. The kind of sheep and the place from which the wool is clipped make a difference: the wool around the shoulders is best—that on the back is worn and often full of burs. A spinner at Log Cabin Village later told

us she got her wool from the Fort Worth zoo across the way, a nice variety and very good, clean wool it is.

MAY 9

1975— On Greer Island, as we waited to lead school children on the trails, the principal told me when he was a boy in Bosque County they had plenty of armadillos. You can try pulling an armadillo out of its hole, but it has a way of hunching its back against the top of its burrow to foil you. Goose the beast, it will quite hunching. But that poses a problem: if you goose with one hand, the other isn't strong enough to pull the animal out by itself; it takes the strength of both arms. In that short free instant when you let go with one hand, it can dig deeper.

MAY 10

1974— Fred and I walked down to see the cliff swallow nests under Belknap Bridge, and there we disturbed a large bullsnake, which no doubt was fattening on fallen nestlings. We admired the dignified way in which the snake threw himself into reverse and slowly withdrew into the hole from which he had half-emerged: it appeared he had simply over-extended himself and now decided to contract. It would be a mistake

to say such art is effortless: rather, it is the apotheosis of effort, action of such economy and joy-of-being as to be a law of motion, a dynamic of life itself.

MAY 11

1977— The morning mail tells me
the world is full of saviors,
albeit none can guarantee
to accomplish salvation
without I send more money.

MAY 12

1967— The Swainson thrush has been fluting his little strangled bugle call from the red mulberry tree now several days. It is much like the wood thrush's call in quality, but reduced in an echo chamber, to a mere whisper. Still, it is an unmistakable signature of one week in May, which I have hardly heard at any other time.

MAY 13

1977— I am really not forgetful,
though sometimes I have to feel
my toothbrush to see if it's wet or dry

before I can tell if I've already brushed.
Besides, my dear wife
admits doing the same.

MAY 14

1974— Went with the Joe Loweses to Cedar Valley, near
Glen Rose, to look for the Golden-Cheeked warbler. A beautiful day, with low-scudding clouds, and the hills bright with
flowers, ranging from minute frog fruit to giant fluttermill
primroses. Painted buntings sang continuously, but we saw
no sign of the Golden-Cheeked until we stopped in a clearing
in the cedar brush in the lee of a small hill and played the
magnetic taped owl call. In short order a frenzy of birds came
to the summons—summer tanagers, black-capped vireos,
Carolina wrens, and at least three Golden-Cheeked warblers.
The call is ghoulish: no wonder it rouses the small-feathered
to fury.

MAY 15

1984— I went to a pharmacy to check my blood pressure,
being alarmed at the reading I had just made at a grocery,
where I had taken it without resting first. Here I sat down
beside a black woman and read a magazine. She had a friend,

another black woman in her sixties, sitting on the only other bench. A white man about our age came in and took a reading on the machine, then turned to the first black woman. "I'm going to live to a hundred and ten," he said. Then he added "And I'm going to drink a lot of whiskey and mess around with women." The black women chuckled. The older one said, "You gonna *think* about messing with women." He then told of a black man, a hundred years old, who lives up on the black cemetery property on 28th Street. That hundred-year-old man still did some patting, and you know why he was able? He eats some greens and some fruit every day.

MAY 16

1969— No discovery like coming upon
for the first time, a rich and generous mind:
one filled with its own peculiar perspective,
opening broad dimensions, disclosing a unique
interior landscape.

MAY 17

1983— As I chopped away with an axe and pick at the rotting stump—all that is left of the magnificent white poplar I planted many years ago in our backyard—I exposed a huge

white borer. A little later, still another, even larger. Both had that curious tapered construction, with regular constrictions at intervals; they had massive, blunt heads, in the center of which were their mandibles. These were the villains, I suppose, that killed the great tree, for I take them to be the larvae of the cottonwood beetle. I left them on the grass to be recycled by some grateful grackle.

MAY 18

1976— No one knows fullness of life who has missed the sensual delight of grappling for potatoes. Grappling is the right word, though it calls for a degree of skill only a little above groping. Into the soft earth the bare hand pushes—it cannot thrust as into looser matter and needs a measure of clawing and poking to be successful. A soil well protected by thick mulch, and particularly a sandy, friable loam such as in my garden will lend itself best to the venture. The hand comes to know what to seek: a firmness in the yielding darkness at the base of green vines (did I say grappling must be done before the plant has begun to wither?), a lumpishness under the fingertips the size of a small box turtle's shell. No doubt of it, it is your potato, as red and thin-skinned as a newborn infant when you learn the joy of ushering it into the

light of day. The experience will repay the new gardener all
toil. Akin, surely, to a father's participation at the bedside
when his first child is brought forth.

MAY 19

1972— In the evening I pick all the berries
　　　　that have turned black or nearly so,
　　　　yet next morning, by a magic I don't understand,
　　　　as many more pebbly fruits have turned.
　　　　This bush, the Brazos berry, so fiendishly thorny,
　　　　it will not give up richness easily.
　　　　I learn to grasp a branch by a leaf
　　　　to steer it aside. Immodestly, I lift a drooping limb
　　　　to see what might be concealed. Every day now
　　　　this clump of bushes yields half a dish,
　　　　and tonight I collect enough for a pie.

MAY 20

1957— My youngest caught a dozen or so horned toads, and
I turned them loose in a flower bed to keep them from dying.
They seemed in a torpor in the box, but once loose, several
displayed what I took to be a sexual frenzy. The males
mounted females, and the latter extended their tails and

gasped. The lizards had clambered about the wire of the box, where I could see their toes were clawed like those of birds.

MAY 21

1955— A rarity—a day of downpours and of creeks and barrow ditches twisting and rushing with brown waters. We have not seen such rain in six years. There is a mesquite pasture with water standing in sheets; an oat field with bales of straw surrounded by pools. The skies are not done with menacing by any means. Drooping keels of clouds fraying into rain pass over us and form an armada in the east that seems eager to turn and deliver yet another barrage. But the rains come too late for gardens, and so late as to ruin the harvest of grains.

MAY 22

1989— This morning I heard a sparrow chirping in the bushes below our second-story bedroom. A monotonous, single chirp, repeated at the same constant interval so often I began counting. He did not stop until I had counted 560 times. Three or four times he wavered—I thought he was stopping, as though his syrinx or whatever apparatus he uses for making noise, had given out. But after a short series he resumed his original sound.

MAY 23

1981— At the Van Cliburn competition I think: this is the Apotheosis of the Hand—nowhere else in all the accomplishments of Humanity can those ten fingers dance so madly, execute so cleanly, move so independently (so it seems) of mind and memory and printed page. Only the passion of the player inhabits those bones, those tendons, those nerves, those muscles. They have formed a partnership with spirit—there are no slaves here. It is as if a great complex of sound had been shattered into delicate fragments, and the cunning fingers ply among the keys, sorting it back together in Space and Time.

MAY 24

1974— The leaves of the prickly ash on Greer Island were covered with yellow spots that looked under a glass to be clumps of butterfly eggs. They may be those of the famous orange dog, which Peattie says gives rise to a butterfly able to radiate its image on a photographic film in absolute darkness. What an artful accomplishment—to give off light even though nobody around can perceive it.

MAY 25

1955— The foliage of the sky today would tax a classic botanist. There are furls and crumpets, and bones and slivers, meringue and cream puffs. North is a dark Niagara and west a far-offishness and vista where the sun gives off a strangely dulled radiance. No artist would dare put into a canvas the hodgepodge of shapes and hues and contrasts found here.

MAY 26

1956— Lower Main Street—always a scenic place. A poor old drunken trollop is being pulled across the street by a big man, perhaps her son, for he seems to be gentle with her. She is crying, "Lemme put my damn shoe on. Lemme put my damn shoe on." One foot is bare and she is holding a shoe in her hand. Finally, she throws it violently, and she stands in the entrance to a cheap hotel while he goes inside alone. A block up the street a man talks with his fingers to two friends. Farther up the way, the dark news vendor, one leg cut off at the knee, cigarette drooping from his lip, sits morosely.

MAY 27

1977— Someone had brought a black vulture of fair size to the Nature Center for rehabilitation. It was hopping around

on the walks, following our group, and had an especial affinity for shoelaces and any strings hanging loose from old jeans. Also, it had the temerity to peck one lady on the seat (she had stooped to pet the baby beaver at the time). I told her it was an Italian buzzard. It ran with an odd loping gait or hop, and was really a clean, respectable pet.

MAY 28
1966— As I waited for the bass player outside Scott Theater, I saw two clouds of midges whirling in their dizzy aerial dance near an abelia hedge. Why did they choose one small pocket of the firmament to whirl in?—for though at times their seething broke apart, they quickly returned to the same cubic yard. Perhaps the perfume of their frenzy maddened the air in that particular spot, making it irresistible. Looking at them and thinking incredulously how they are able to avoid collisions (even as whirligig beetles on water), I came again to relativity. To some slow monster on the edge of space, our solar year would be no more than a spin in a dervish dance.

MAY 29
1974— Another thing fingernails are good for
            is snapping beans.

Clearly, the thumbnail is specifically designed
for taking off the end of a beanpod cleanly, briskly.
How Evolution arranged this
I have no idea.

MAY 30

1963— Somewhere in the neighborhood a mourning dove
hoots, the first gasping sob like that of a lost woman.

MAY 31

1962— The fledgling blue jay in our backyard has not yet
formed his topknot, but his head is a rich velvet knob. He
squawks at intervals and then sits with his eyes closed sleep-
ily. Another, more active, tries to crack a pecan he has found
among fallen leaves. He holds it with his toes against a branch
and pecks away.

JUNE

JUNE 1

1976— Tonight, without any warning, a patch of skin on the sole of my left foot has come loose and needs peeling off. No cause for alarm: such has happened through the years (I've never kept count whether it recurred every seven years, as they told me it would when I was a boy). Well, I'm ready for a whole new hide, inside and out. Trouble is, skin doesn't change when it renews itself—even the fingerprints stay the same. A snake, a toad, a cicada, a man, how does anyone go about revamping the heart or the brain?

JUNE 2

1975— It is manifestly unfair to call some flowers "false"— false dandelion, false gaura, and the like—merely because they resemble some earlier discovery. Yet this is the way the human mind must work, from the resemblance to another until distinctions are picked up. Only Sunday I told a fellow how much he looked like so-and-so.

JUNE 3

1973—   The after-thunder is the most lyrical.
        Rumbling that bruits a coming storm
        carries a menace that distracts the ear:

preparations must be made,
both house and mind must be battened down
before fury strikes,
the enormous rhythms cannot be enjoyed.
At the height of the storm strokes come too rapid,
overlapping, shouting in disconcord.
But when the crest has passed over
the ear learns the meaning of reverberation.
Listen. A single surge of thunder
unfolds its distinctive pattern to the mind,
a jagged motif full of projections, notches.
There—it repeats itself in another key,
again, again, the profile distinguishable
if you harken fiercely—six, seven times,
till finally at the very edge of earth
it shakes the foundations of Creation.

JUNE 4

1968— At New Salem Park, Illinois, a rose-breasted gros-
beak called in a tree near us as we made camp. Red-headed
woodpeckers lighted up the shade with their whiteness; robins, cowbirds, catbirds, white-breasted nuthatches showed. I
was watching a redhead when a small boy came down the
trail, asked me what I was doing. I told him, saying we didn't

have many of these where I came from. "Well, you'd better look at me," he said. I did, for the first time. He had bright red hair and a big smile, and I touseled the hair and told his parents what he had said.

JUNE 5
1958— Nothing fascinates me more than watching the inhabitants of the vitex bush when it is in flower. A butterfly with blue-black wings and red chevrons stands with its suction pump at work. Several smaller engage in a dogfight above the highest branches—I even saw one pursue a sparrow that flew over. As many as four of them whirl in a wild hurly-burly of dodging and weaving and twisting flight. These for the most part are of orange and white polka dot design. I find myself wishing there were a more fitting name for the butterfly—something describing this absolutely frenzied yet well-controlled flight. Those wings perform maneuvers a man cannot imagine; he can only observe.

JUNE 6
1976— You, Lady,
        are a collection of lyrics,
        beside whom other women
        are mere reference books.

JUNE 7

1980— To gather beans in comfort, a bean-picker needs first of all a two-gallon metal bucket. This, not to put beans in but to put the posterior on, for the picker will find stooping or squatting between bushes a great strain on the enthusiasm. No, the bucket must be turned upside down between rows, where it forms an admirable seat. Its mouth holds firmly on loose soil and does not give way treacherously as a stool might. There is something fitting about using a receptacle in this reverse manner in order to accumulate a harvest. It shows that a man need not be cowed by his contrivances, and may use them however suits him.

JUNE 8

1951— A sudden fierce branch of lightning runs through the eastern edge of night. And as I look and the flaring dies in my eyes, there goes a solitary firefly wandering in the rain.

JUNE 9

1970— On the Freeway:
> The way around the jackass in front—
> why is it always blocked
> by the jackrabbit, hell-bent,
> coming around your own behind?

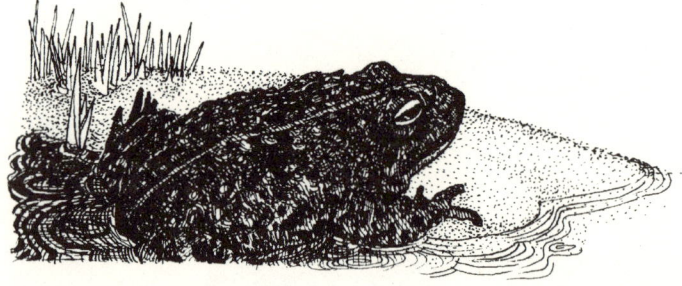

JUNE 10

1974— We had to rise very early to get to the wharf in Sausalito in time for the pelagic trip. Going under Golden Gate Bridge was magnificent. We saw common murres, California gulls, Heerman gulls, Western gulls, pelagic cormorants, Brandts cormorants, most of them running across the water into flight as our yacht came close. The upper structure of the bridge was clothed in fog as we went out, but it was really a good day, we understood. I noted that the murres and cormorants flew in lines. The farther we went the more I realized I was going to become seasick—and worst of all, I also realized that we were only started, had the whole day before us. Commodore Barney, if he was really any kin, must have turned his head while he watched my stomach turn. I was not the only one sick: several were stretched out in bunks much of the trip. At the Farallones we saw tufted puffins, black oystercatchers, sooty shearwaters, common scoters, pigeon guillemots, Stellers sealions; white pelicans later near Alcatraz. I thought we saw brown pelicans also. We came back about 2 P.M. in order to avoid the fog which rolls in shortly thereafter. Once back on solid ground we felt normal enough (Mary never was very much nauseated, but I retched a half dozen times or more).

JUNE 11

1969— We move out of an era of discovery into one
of consolidating gains, licking our sores,
refreshing our psyches—whatever people do
to restore themselves after overexertion.
The ticker tape is running far behind.
The artist must slow down his pace.
The human mind is surfeited with the new,
the strange, the hurtful, the unthinkable.
Knowledge, like wine, requires aging
and the arts thrive best on decaying matter.

JUNE 12

1975—One of the world's most beautiful creatures sleeps
under bridges. I never see him perched there that I do not
marvel at his coloration, nor see him scudding low over mead-
ows and ditches without delighting in his supple motion, that
sheer bravura of barn swallow.

JUNE 13

1955— There could be no finer moment than that we spent
together picking beans. We made a race out of it, who should
find the longest beanpod. He trampled over my vines with

fine disregard, and I warned him repeatedly. But what were bean vines compared with enthusiasm? While chopping away at weeds with a hoe, he banged me across the shins. I howled. "Why don't you watch what you're doing?" I moaned. "Well, why don't you get out of the way?" There was nothing impertinent about his saying. To him, obviously, the simple logic of the matter was that I intruded on his scheme of things. I tried lamely to convince him that he was helping me and should be more careful. Who knows what impression all this fatherly wisdom made?

JUNE 14

1979— The toad, though he molt his skin
      a thousand times, will still be a toad.
      A man ought to be a kind of toad
      who somewhere has learned to pass
      through being skinned alive, to come forth
      a higher creature.

JUNE 15

1955— I will remember the orange glow of the sky last night and the strange color it lent to the vitex blooms. The tree is at its height of blossom, with hundreds of long tapering spikes

of blue. The evening sky touched it with something unearthly. Moreover, it displayed one of those rare cloud formations consisting of many little pots of paint hung in the air.

JUNE 16

1944— I dug out the old official diary in which I recorded one of the more memorable days in my short career as a post office inspector. It was June 16, 1944. What made it memorable was the use of nine different vehicles (counting shank's mare) to accomplish the day's work. To begin with, I rode with Inspector E. E. English from Rio Grande City to Garciasville, where I inspected the office alone; then with the star route carrier, a Mr. Naranja, whose handsome mustache, expressive shrug, and knowledge of the thorny plants of the chaparral through which we dodged I remember well— to Los Ebanos, another inspection; then by a special conveyance (the required term in an expense account; it was actually an old jalopy), back to the main highway; by bus to the La Joya stop; by another conveyance to the La Joya post office, where I discovered a technical problem in the books. This upset some delicate timing. I walked back to the bus stop, but at 5:40 P.M., the last bus going west had run. I thumbed a ride with a citizen to Sullivan City, where I stood across from

a small cafe wondering how I would get back to Rio Grande City before dark, or ever.

A border patrol car stopped at the cafe and I walked over and showed my commission to two officers. Sorry, they were not going west. When they finished their meal and came back out, they saw me still standing forlornly holding my leather briefcase and waving my free thumb. They called to me to come get in their vehicle; shortly, a pipe truck came from the east and they turned their siren on and brought him to a stop. The driver was happy to discover he was getting only a passenger, not a ticket. Thus, I finally arrived at Rio Grande City at 7:45 P.M. For the day I spent $1.85 for meals, $2.50 for lodging, and 80 cents for various rides. Looking back, I see this hardly conveys the charm of the whole adventure, most of which, I suspect, has arisen in hindsight.

JUNE 17

1969— In J. W. Wells Park in Michigan we found much to enjoy: redstarts, a Baltimore oriole, tree swallows. In one drinking fountain a bird had built a nest—we were in the first wave of campers. Nearby were strange squarish ferns. Looked at from above, the fronds formed squares. Of these two things I promised myself to take pictures, but in the morning a bitter cold rain sent us packing.

JUNE 18

1951— On a downtown street corner, the blind man sang "Mockingbird Hill" as he played his accordion: "Tra-la-la-fiddle-dee-dee-dee!"

JUNE 19

1958— The postmaster at Edgewood, the Tomato Town, says farmers no longer take their produce to Dallas. They can do as well or better selling by the roadside. That way, too, there is no wear and tear on the pickup, and the old man is not so likely to drink up all the profits overnight in Dallas.

JUNE 20

1981— Our resident mockingbird the other night,
    a moonlit one, was giving us a fine performance
    when he fell to repeating a single long note,
    just such a note as bobwhites sometimes call.
    He repeated it so many times I started counting,
    reached twenty-five before he quit.
    He must have done it fifty times, all told.
    Is there a Guinness Book for mockingbirds?

JUNE 21

1983— It is truly summer in our city now, for I see the young little blue herons, in their snow-white plumage, flying over the downtown skyscrapers as they go out to forage from the herony at the foot of Paddock Viaduct. My brother-in-law, J. D. White, discovered this herony when he was climbing in the superstructure of the Texas Electric plant. He asked me what they were; I had no idea until I went to see for myself. Dozens of nesting little blue herons and cattle egrets in a grove protected by fences of the American Cyanimide plant! The local Audubon Society was overjoyed.

JUNE 22

1977— The orderliness of an ear of corn—
       you have to look close to appreciate.
       Those kernels are not stacked
       in vertical ranks around the cob:
       they're cunningly laid with rounded corners,
       each tucked snugly over gaps below
       like courses of brick.
       If I peer closely I can see
       the lines wind slowly in a spiral
       like worshippers up to a mountain shrine.

JUNE 23

1976— Today I tried tongs to pluck the spotted beetles from my horseradish. I had a choice of three instruments: two tweezers and one of Mary's hair clips. The hair clip worked almost to perfection once I learned how to use it. You cannot lunge for the bug like a heron spearing fish, but must rather sidle up to it with jaws agape and catch it midway in the V. The same bugs, though, showed up on my almost defunct broccoli and collards. One look at the swarms of them there, and I gave up tong warfare.

JUNE 24

1975— I don't know why, but the thought
            came into my mind:
            was the Snake in the Garden of the venemous kind?
            Somehow I always thought of him
            as a sort of boa constrictor.

JUNE 25

1976— Before dawn I heard a low sound.
            Was it my stomach cooing,
            that strange, repetitive gargle?
            No, it turned out to be a yellow-billed cuckoo

pumping away at a muffled note
in the pecan tree outside my window.

JUNE 26

1976— The garden boasts only one sizable dill plant this
year—none of the seed I planted came up, and this one vol-
unteered. It is a thing of umbelliferous beauty, heavy with
seed, and yesterday I found four magnificent marauders—
tiger-striped caterpillars that looked like pictures I have seen
of swallowtail larvae. They munched away, and I couldn't
bring myself to kill such striking creatures. As I scraped them
off the dill with the point of a knife, their feathery orange
antennae shot out in alarm and they held to the stem with
their stubby paws. I left them in a can a few yards away, and
they were soon crawling out. They have at least a fighting
chance to find their way back to the dill, or to learn to eat
mustard.

JUNE 27

1968— We are chemists who test and test
the substances with which we deal, and discover
in a few years or days or hours before it is gone
what its real value is. As though we are candles

pulling from our sides the precious stuff of life
to offer up to the feeding flame
in order that we may see
what manner of candles we are.

JUNE 28

1977— Today I ground soybeans toward making tempeh, and
I took advantage of a stout south breeze to winnow the hulls.
I don't know exactly why, nor do I care much to have a rea-
son but the act of winnowing made me feel heroic.

JUNE 29

1972— I doubt if the cicada
gives out his rasping chatter because of an urge
to express himself. No, he has only heard
some other cicada, and he has to respond,
has to vibrate to the rhythm of peers.
And that second cicada heard another, and so on
down
to one that began the morning chorus
thinking he'd heard.

JUNE 30

1952— Under the Brazos River bridge at Granbury we found a cluster of harvesters—daddy longlegs we called them. They stood so motionless I thought them dead, but at a touch some of them bounded off like little living shock-absorbers in action.

JULY

JULY 1

1974— Between the arching trees over the road by the river
it is never utterly still:
leaves fall prematurely, willow and cottonwood fluff
float in the air both upward and downward;
gossamers give way.
At times small birds or erratic
dragonflies
break the tranquility.
Even while I jot these words
a small beetle lights and crawls over the page.

JULY 2

1971— I like to sit watching Bermuda grass
spring back into place where my foot has crushed it.
Blade by blade, stem by stem, like clockwork,
it regains its original condition.
Being stepped on interlocks it
into a three-dimensional jigsaw mix
which it has to solve, piece by piece;
a blade must give way here
before the one beneath can click into place.
Over the width of a shoe motions take turns,

now at this side, now another yonder.
It is a picture of resurgence,
of life fighting back after taking a blow.
Watched long enough, the grass will return
to its fullest deployment.
The cost of observing this heroic struggle
is practically nothing.

JULY 3

1979— Yesterday, another great Black-Eyed Pea Day. We went again, Mary and I, to the Conwell Farm in Azle, to buy black-eyed peas, prepared to pick them if we had to. The farmer was storming about a boy he had kept through the winter, who had quit him the day before, just when the peas needed picking. He took us by pickup truck down a rough sandy road to the pea field, where several pickers were already at work, a white couple and a black. We were invited to take two rows and pick to both ends, about four hundred feet in length. It did not take that much to fill two bushel baskets. The farmer left, returned, and left again before we were through.

It was pleasant in the field, a south breeze blowing. We carefully avoided the bull nettle that bloomed here and there

in the rows. Occasionally a bobwhite called, or a yellow-billed cuckoo gurgled. The elderly white woman complained about her back, said she had picked twelve bushels last year, filled her freezer, and given away peas to her son. But she told him she didn't love him that much this year.

Coming home, I set about running the peas through the new pea-sheller; after several adjustments in the arrangements of pans, I found the optimum method and by 8 P.M. the shelling was done, compared with past midnight last year. Neither of us understands why this menial work is so satisfying. Perhaps one reason is knowing that we do not have to do it. Another, that it takes us out of our city surroundings and gives us a taste of what it would be like if we had to live by what we could take from the soil.

JULY 4

1976— The Glorious Bicentennial Fourth
We went early, about 7 P.M. to the new Heritage Park below the jail, hoping to see the balloon ascensions at eight o'clock and also to be on hand timely to form ranks for the Bicentennial Volunteer Chorus. The symphony would play before us, and then under John Giordano we would sing "Memories of America," an arrangment by Carmen Dragon—which we had

rehearsed valiantly. NBC had its batteries of lights ready, and around 8:30 P.M., the national network would cut to Fort Worth.

The north levee of the Trinity River was crowded with people, as was the bluff behind us. In the flood plain, at the confluence of the forks of the river, thousands of people milled or sat waiting on bales of straw brought in for seats. On the far side of the Trinity a space had been reserved for a monster fireworks display at the conclusion of the program. All sorts of humanity continued to stream into the new park, and without exception, all presented their happiest faces. A spirit of hope, of a desire to shake off the last few years of troubled history, seemed to pervade us. I have never seen a more joyful multitude.

The day before, it had rained heavily, and the clouds let us know that more rain would come. Nobody backed down from the threat, even though weather forecasters mentioned heavy rains thirty miles to the south of the Metroplex. As the night came on the clouds became heavier. At 8 P.M. Winston excitedly called my attention to a small cloud, like a funnel, dropping down from a huge sliding plow of nimbostratus in the northeast. If it was a funnel cloud, it disturbed no one. Everybody in Texas knows that tornadoes travel toward the northeast, not from—well, most of the time. Still,

we could now see a downpour beginning east of the city. The whole system moved slowly toward us.

John Giordano no more than anyone else had any saving plan of what to do in case of rain. He finally decided to beat its arrival and called for the concluding number, the "Memories of America" by the chorus. The "A" for tuning sounded on a trumpet, but it was too late, rain began to fall in huge drops. All those expensive violins and delicate woodwinds! He turned to the microphone and shouted for everybody to take cover.

Cover? There wasn't enough real cover to shelter five hundred bodies, let alone unnumbered thousands caught in a deluge. We huddled miserably on the risers, trying to keep musical scores dry. The orchestra scrambled their instruments into cases and fled from the stage. The Shrine Band, unafraid of wetting their brass, struck up "Dixie," and a rousing cheer went up from soaked heads. This plainly was the end of the concert. We went to find Mary and the two granddaughters and, if possible, cover for them. We stood next to a temporary building first, then by a truck that diverted some of the torrent. Elizabeth and the girls tried to fend off the downpour with folding chairs we had brought for sitting. The girls even sought shelter in the folds of the colonial dress Mary had so proudly made and worn for the occasion.

An excited voice warned the crowd to stay away from the steel towers supporting the television lights, and the power cables running to them. But drenched men and women paid little attention. Anywhere protection offered, they huddled. The subway stop became solid with compressed human flesh. The space under the risers for the chorus likewise, though it leaked.

Finally, we had enough. The rain showed no sign of diminishing. We agreed the symphony would never return, that the fireworks display could not possibly come off. We turned our soggy backs on Heritage Park and struck out for our car a half mile away. As we walked toward the base of the bluff, a sheet of water sluiced downhill around our feet. Violent thunder and frequent flashes of lightning constantly reminded us of a very real danger—if lightning had struck anywhere among all those wet feet, some of us would have sizzled.

Before we left the bottom we passed by one of the long strings of portable toilets, and we saw they too were crammed with people seeking shelter. Elizabeth said she counted five bodies in one, and Lord knows they scarcely accommodate a single on proper occasions.

Slogging up the bluff on Taylor Street proved great fun,

for here the stream of people converged and fought its way up against the stream of water pouring down the pavement. At one place two young men abandoned themselves to the elements and began sliding down the gutter at the east side where the main drainage gushed a foot or so deep. All around us we heard laughter and cries of "Happy Birthday!" Not even being half-drowned was going to ruin the high moment for most. I heard only one murmur against the turn of affairs (aside from the complaints of two disappointed granddaughters). A woman behind me on the chorus risers, when it began to rain, had muttered darkly, "This is tacky!"

Cindy had to be constantly reassured. She was scared. I consoled her by explaining that as long as she could see the lightning there was nothing to be afraid of, but if it actually struck her she would never know it. She wasn't content with only one adult holding a hand. She wanted two hand-holders.

We drove home and shucked our wet clothes, wet stockings, wet shoes. It was over, and we would keep an ear open in case the rain, now dying away, gave a respite and a few fireworks became possible. Winston called a bit later saying they had decided to return, just in case, but I thought and said No, it's all over. But it wasn't. We began to hear the

boom of fireworks. We dressed hurriedly and drove the short distance to downtown. Sure enough, there were blossoms in the sky over the Texas Electric plant.

Oddly, large spaces on the asphalt paving in the park had dried quickly. Mary and I sat down to watch. A perfect evening. The moon had come out and stars, though in the west an angry quaking of lightning continued. Friends came by who had endured all and were still soaked. We learned that in our absence the remains of the chorus had regrouped and rendered, a cappella, the Dragon number. Good for them and shame on us.

In the end the fireworks too had to be abridged because prepared displays had gotten wet. The final shot into the sky went enormously high and left persistent little puffs of white that stayed and stayed. Slowly, reluctantly, the onlookers decided it was truly all over. They began to drift toward the bluff, still cheerful, though many sloshed along in wet shoes. If anything, a sense of regret, of hating to see such a beautiful day come to an end, emanated from them.

On this same day other cities in the land held their celebrations, in which everything went off just as men and women had planned for months, even years. I felt rather sorry for them. How many would have Memories of America like

ours? How many could compare in unforgettableness, with our wet symphony and chorus, our vast crowd of happy, miserably drenched partakers slogging in ankle-deep retreat out of the deluge, or watching our belated bombs bursting in air with thistle-ball after thistle-ball of magnificent, exploding fire?

JULY 5

1969— So far as I can tell
the world can do quite handily without me
though I'm not anxious to put it to the test.
I have a notion eternity
may not find me indispensable.
I will try to leave a small fossil,
but what is to keep it too from being buried
by yet another inland sea?

JULY 6

1974— The dill planted in my garden has made seed
despite drouth and the ravages of two caterpillars
I plucked from it. What a strange pleasure
to know dill intimately for the first time!
to roll the twigs in my palms, dislodging aromatic
grain.

When the harvest is completed, behold, the perfect
    outline
of a compound umbel naked in my hand!
From a central stalk arch a dozen fine green stems,
at the end of each, at the most pleasant point of curve,
suddenly other, smaller crowns of jet appear—
and all disposed in exquisite order
to round out the master umbel.
Men can make a fountain, no doubt of that,
but they can never match this ingenuity—
a spray that elaborates at the tip-ends
like the primordial life-cell
into small replicas of itself.

JULY 7

1968— At Ludington, Michigan State Park, on the island trail at about 5:30 A.M., I was standing quietly when a mink moved toward me. He did not see or scent me, and I watched him sniffing more or less contentedly here and there. He did not seem ferocious to me—perhaps he had already found some squirrel or spermophile. When I did move he tried vainly to scent me, wrinkling his nose; but his vision, though I was only a few feet away, did him little good.

JULY 8

1963— Brazos River: Painted buntings sing everywhere, all day long. They especially like uppermost branches of dead trees. The song is a sweet whistling of rising and falling notes, almost a slow trill. The peewees are in good number, singing pee-wee! pee-urr! in the early morning and at night. Chuck-will's-widows sound at night, and I catch a glimpse of one in the twilight before they begin their concert. Indian blanket is mostly gone, with the red rays falling away from duller globes, like cooling suns; ironweed with purple blossoms is everywhere, and butterflies of all descriptions are having a field day among them. Ronald points out the logarithmic spiral of the sunflower disks (actually, double spirals). Strange how so many plants in this river bottom are aromatic. Crush the croton and you find it almost as strong as horsemint. The camphor weed if pressed smells a little like camphor, mostly like itself. In addition, a rough shrub, very thorny, has a leaf that smells like kerosene when you bruise it. It makes me wonder if people raised in these bottoms are not similar—nondescript on the surface but full of tang if bruised?

JULY 9

1963— We bathed in the shallow rapids by full moon. I caught a beautiful smile on Mary's face as she reveled in the loveliness of the scene. Later, though, after our family took to cots, a wild gang of drunken teenagers, boys and girls, came down to swim. Their curses and obscenities and giggles filled the hours until very late. I had some notion there might be trouble, but they did not bother us.

JULY 10

1968— Once more I find the keys
     of my typewriter piled.
     But now it is a granddaughter
     who cannot resist this machine
     which thinks it stitches, bit by bit,
     patches meant to make sense.

JULY 11

1955— There is really something a little ridiculous about a cattleguard. To see a brute animal foiled by such a simple device is sad. But it is true of barbed wire too. What trifles dismay beasts into submission. It would be a matter for irony

if I did not remember that I also allow myself to be hedged in with hints, with the merest suggestion of difficulties. Is a horse ever worried whether a frayed shirt sleeve will make him a social outcast?

JULY 12

1965— Mimosas rain gently against the light of the descending sun as we sit at the table in the backyard eating our supper. This is not weeping: it is profligacy for a tree to give up moisture in this cruel month of July. But I can see the drops steadily falling as the leaves begin to close. The expressions of this graceful plant have pleased me more than the fruit of my pecan trees, diseased or insect-ruined as they usually are.

JULY 13

1976— It must have been in July when Phil Sheridan said, "If I owned Hell and Texas, I would sell Texas and move to Hell." Yes, but who in Hell would want to buy Texas in July?

JULY 14

1957— Driving through Hill County, even above the odors of the auto, I can smell the scent of acres of horsemint.

JULY 15

1969— In the space between summer and autumn
come brittle moments, when the fate of the season
hangs in the balance,
to be decided by the smallest of weights.
And it comes, inevitably it comes:
even now a leaf is cutting at its hawser.

JULY 16

1977— It is not that the spiders
have suddenly in a frenzy
begun weaving webs wherever places can be
found—
it is only that the mist
has made their usual pursuit
visible. So says the book.
I wonder: does the web's being easily seen
make warier prey, hungrier spiders?

JULY 17

1968— As we went over the Air Mail Facility site at the
new Houston airport, a family of killdeer was also inspect-
ing the place. Two tiny chicks, probably just hatched, ran

out in the street, and the parents fluttered about anxiously as our car came near. When we got out, the chicks scampered to the curb and one of them crouched down in obedience to some call from the mother. The latter began her broken wing act by lying flat on the ground and wagging her wings piteously. At the same time she repeated a little piping tone continuously. When I went to look for the chicks, they had frozen into invisibility.

JULY 18

1972— I once put a mole in a bucket of water
　　　　where he paddled till exhausted and then drowned.
　　　　It wasn't out of cruelty, but squeamishness—
　　　　I didn't have the fortitude to kill him outright.
　　　　I should have thought of carrying him off some-
　　　　　　　where,
　　　　far enough from my lawn, and letting him live.
　　　　As it is, I still carry the picture in my mind
　　　　of that poor creature scraping and paddling
　　　　with his great useless claws at the tin sides
　　　　of the pail. I cannot purge my memory
　　　　of all the stupidities I have done.

JULY 19

1976— If I could only raise such a garden
        as when my generous wife
        gives the increase to kin and neighbors
        I would not feel robbed.

JULY 20

1979— Horses have enough sense to stand head to tail and swat each other's flies, but I have never seen cows or bulls do the same. They just don't seem very intelligent. Maybe this is one reason why we eat beef, but not horseflesh.

JULY 21

1960— On two occasions we cooked out in Boulder Canyon. A mountain stream overflowing from the reservoir at Nederland rushes along the floor of the canyon, and it is right to call it icy cold, for it is directly from melting snowbanks on the mountains to the west. The sides of the canyon are frequently sheer rock, occasionally timbered or scrubby; at times with enough soil to permit wild flowers in profusion. Let the eye dwell on the rocks for only a minute and small movements that are chipmunks make themselves evident. They are scarcely larger than mice, short-tailed, very brisk, not too fearful. There are few birds in the depth of the can-

yon. Early on one morning we saw three deer, very near the outskirts of the city. We saw so many things to refresh our arid eyes—wild roses, strawberries, flowers we could not name, ferns, mosses in rounded masses streaking the cliffs, lichens bright of hue and pure. I should propose to compare my own character with that of lichens—not particularly or not at all noticeable for color unless you look, not particularly useful except to break down rock into soil that will feed the valleys below (a noble enough self-portrait).

JULY 22

1976— Another cause
for women libbers to protest—
all the little Bicentennial fire hydrants
painted so brightly in our town
are obviously boys.

JULY 23

1972— A Carolina wren is loose in our neighborhood,
the first I remember ever in these parts.
Is that not worth spreading news of?
But no need. He does his own bugling well enough.
So tiny a bird, such a welkinful of sound.

JULY 24

1952— At Granite Mountain a great deafening saw with multiple blades cut at several slabs at once, water spewing on each cut. I tried to talk to the old man tending the saw, but we could not understand each other for the noise. Out of this vast dome the State Capitol, our own Tarrant County Courthouse, the seawall at Galveston, and many other structures in Texas have come, and hardly a dent has been made in the pink lump.

JULY 25

1969— Some bird cries
though hardly outbursts of pure lyricy
serve surely as splendid punctuation
fitting the spaces of silence together.

JULY 26

1952— Llano River: The granite shoals, a network of rivulets threading at all angles and working themselves over the masses of stone rounded and scooped and sculpted by years of waters. Gar heads and skins here and there, showing that disgusted fishermen preceded us. Fat, brawny grasshoppers in the sunflowers on the bank eluded me consistently, know-

ing just when to tick and scrape off to a new lodging place.
Sandpipers ran on the sandbars. Rabbits jumped and tusseled
in the brush. The boys rousted a skunk in its travels. At a
waterhole a cow and her calf came across the dry creekbed
and stood looking at me uncertainly for a long time. Their
trail down to the water wound through high weeds and among
the woods, skirting outcrops of granite wherever possible.

JULY 27

1977 — Mary and I watched it lightning from our front porch
        as a tremendous storm roared over the city.
       Two kinds of lightning played:
       long, brilliant, crooked columns
       that stood in the southeastern sky
       for incredibly long moments,
       and general flashes that filled the whole sector.
       I noticed a strange phenomenon:
       with every one of those bright strokes
       an afterimage stood in my retina
       for seconds on end. And if a sky-filling flash
       followed in that time, the image-stroke
       stood out as a dark shadow, a sort of black
          lightning,

a negative of the white that had vanished.
Once I counted to eighteen
before the shadow disappeared.

JULY 28
1969— I took a picture of the statue in front of the Will
Rogers Coliseum. It is good to live in a town where the only
statue of a man on horseback is that of a cowboy humorist.
A town where the only fort to amount to anything was the
name prefixed as a kind of courtesy to a little-known (now)
general.

JULY 29
1957— We spent two nights on the beach at Rockport, with
the Gulf breeze a blast over us. I thought to separate the mix-
ture of sounds of wind and surf, but going far out on a pier
past the breakers I found it peaceful and quiet. The surf alone
is the roarer. Individual waves become streaked as they curl
over: there are foreriding and afterriding furrows and clefts,
the foam quickly vanishes. But sound never dies.

JULY 30

1955— As our bus goes by, I see a boy of about ten, asleep on top of the cooling box of a watermelon stand at the side of the road. He must have slept there all night, guarding his precious fruit. His quilts bunch behind his neck, his blue-jeaned legs are uncovered. It is, after all, impossible for a boy to stay completely covered.

JULY 31

1988— David Dalager pointed out to me an advantage of being left-handed that I had never heard of. This: that a man turning a screwdriver with his left hand is better equipped for the job because the muscles and formation of the hand accommodate themselves more readily to the action of turning a screw clockwise than do those of a right-handed man. This is one of the rare instances I, a left-hander, know of in which the left hand is more fortunate than the right.

AUGUST

AUGUST 1

1962— From the barge looking down into the waters of Lake Whitney, I cannot hope to say in words what the water is doing: at one time of day, the wind chopping softly, the surface is a constant creation of elliptical mirrors, of blue paint pots, of instant puddles of mercury sliding and spilling together and then apart. One morning the surface rolls in small waves toward the limestone cliffs, and every wave is scaly as a black snake. One evening the mirrors are reflecting in another direction, and a continual calculus takes the eye. The shine is yellowish-green if I look sidelong away from it.

AUGUST 2

1953— The ants gathered about the dead green worm, nuzzling at it like a multitude of pigs against a sow. Occasionally they moved it, so that it seemed to move of itself; but it was dead, and the news of death had gone out over the sidewalk. A fair distance away, a number of outlying groups or systems of the ant population milled excitedly; it seemed they had lost or been unable to establish communication with the center of the feast. I watched solitary insects making hasty loops out and back to the thick of the confusion. Surprisingly, only one ant went in anything like a straight line,

directly across the sidewalk. There always has to be an individualist.

AUGUST 3

1968— How much more secure I feel
        now that I know the name
        of the tomato hornworm on our vitex tree—
        and that of the ox beetle someone put
        on the bookshelf.
        Having names to call them
        drains out some of the horror.

AUGUST 4

1978— The long drouth of June and July made the rubber hose of my windshield wiper brittle until it split, but when I replaced it the washer worked stoutly. I went into the house and triumphantly announced to Mary, "It squirts like a two-year-old boy!" That wise mother of four sons looked at me. "I can think of a better comparison," she said.

AUGUST 5

1974— We went to a farm near Arlington to gather corn and okra and tomatoes for putting up. I stooped to pluck one especially large ripe and red tomato, almost hidden in a dense

gathering of foliage, and suddenly something stirred—a mother quail came fluttering out, crying plaintively. I think it more honest to say she came out weeping, so sorrowful she was: not loud, but almost as if she were overcome with emotion. I looked under the leaves, and there lay a nestful of eggs and a few tiny chicks just emerged from their shells. I had come at a most critical moment. Had I taken the roof off her world? I called Mary to show her and then we moved quickly away so that the mother bird could return. I have sought to convince myself I did no real harm—the shade remained. Perhaps I really removed a threat, that heavy tomato hanging over the nest like a dangerously swollen sun.

AUGUST 6

1972— I hear a blue jay cooing
      softly to another,
      a sleepy telephone
      off the hook.

AUGUST 7

1974— I would not want to go through a life in Texas without paying tribute to the beauty and singular fitness of Spanish words—and Mexican, with their own distinctive flavor. Nor do I care greatly from which source—Arabic, Latin,

Aztec, Mayan—they came. It is enough that golondrina, caballo, lagarto, jagarundi, and ten thousand others exist, each exquisitely shaped and just, fresh from the forge of the human mind, chili-hot.

AUGUST 8
1953— At Fred's pond the small frogs described three sides of an octagon as they hopped away on the mudflat. I managed to swat three of them for bait. They had a trick of lurching to the water's edge but not going in, and I learned finally to strike at that point. Still, I enjoyed seeing these creatures, no bigger than the end of my finger, fly through the air a foot or more high and perhaps two feet at a hop.

AUGUST 9
1972— You cannot keep the cricket of sorrow
      out of your house. He will come and striddle
      by your bedside, in the night,
      while you are untying knots.

AUGUST 10
1988— At Palo Duro Canyon, a warm evening. The people in line to be served barbecue fanned themselves with their

paper plates. In the amphitheater, the girl ushers taking people to their seats tucked up their long dresses (which they wore performing in "Texas") as they mounted the high steps.

AUGUST 11

1977— At the petting zoo sharp-eyed Cindy
called my attention to the llama
chewing its cud:
first on the left side, then on the right,
back and forth, with utmost precision.
Now, is this true of llamas everywhere?
Or was this an especially efficient one,
striving to equalize wear and tear
on both jaws?
The goats in the zoo did not appear
to bother much about which way to chew;
they chomped wherever the cud made its way.

AUGUST 12

1976— A small discovery of mine is a Better Way to Swat Flies. More efficacious, more certain, more deadly. How many of us have swatted at but missed completely? It is not that aim is poor or resolve flawed—technique is lacking. Here,

then, is the Improved Method: With the free hand, hold back the head of the swatter as you approach the suspecting fly. (For he does suspect: he thinks he knows just how swiftly you can levy the blow, and he sits there contemptuous—sure that he can evade your best.) But now, lo, the swatter is already cocked. No preparatory motion is needed. The arrow is strung to the bow: pull back with one hand and snap with the other. Where now is all that contemptuousness? Pulp.

AUGUST 13

1961— While swimming in the surf at Freeport, I saw a piece of seaweed in which something wiggled, and I cupped my hand under it and caught myself a baby flounder, about the diameter of a pencil, dark brown to black in color. As I showed it to the boys, a wave broke over us, and the fish leaked through my fingers and escaped. Looking for it, I chanced to see the forms of larger fish riding in the crests of the surf—I had not known this was their habit. Ronald says there is a warning against diving into waves, because sharks, like other fish, inhabit these crests.

AUGUST 14

1954— Rain over the Guadalupes: The veil of the mountains obscured by the advancing veil of the rain. The storm rinses

the timeless face of El Capitan; what little dust has crumbled from it is now washed away in spates of water rushing down the mountainside. Farther south, we camped in the Davis Mountains where the first white men in this region camped, under three great cottonwoods. The sound of Limpia Creek ran high after rain, but it subsided by morning. Autos going over the cattleguard nearby jarred the silence through the night, and a donkey braying heralded the morning light. I shaved in the mountain stream after a miserable, cold sleep, grateful to see the dawn come slowly.

AUGUST 15

1961— At Gettysburg we were fascinated by the old cemetery that was there long before the battle, particularly by the magnificent trees; most of all, by the giant purple beeches. They looked like creations taken from a tale of trolls, great twisted, almost human-leathery trunk and root and branch. The roots formed basins that held the rain. Only the top of the leaves had the deep brownish purple. There were other strange trees, ginkgo, Sarawak cedar, Norwegian maple. Their size would seem to antedate the great battle. And in the cemetery we found some burial dates in the 1700's, the oldest a flat iron-stone almost flush with the ground.

AUGUST 16

1953— On the breeze out of the south, the sound of the black preacher's voice reaches us through the dark from the revival down in the Trinity bottom. It is a long quaver. I cannot make out the words, but the rise and fall is exhortation enough. And it is a disciplined device, one on which he can call at will.

AUGUST 17

1971—   Some birds sing only at dawn
              or a few notes at dusk.
              Or only deep in a wood, on a mountaintop.
              To hear them, the ear must be brought
              like a cup to the well that is beside
              the gate at Bethlehem.

AUGUST 18

1973— We arrived in Jackson, Wyoming shortly before noon. First saw Tetons a few miles south of the city. We found the school auditorium where Robert was playing and went in to hear the rehearsal. He saw us and smiled. I believe it was on this occasion that we encountered the drunken Indian who had entered the building with a bottle and couldn't seem to

understand where he was and why. But the fortissimo passages excited him: he would stand up and shake and tremble in time, as best he could, and apparently wanted to shout something. Mary finally told him to keep quiet. He did. (Mary actually guided him outside and told some men sitting there that he was making a disturbance, and would they keep him from coming back in. Her version of this is better than mine.)

AUGUST 19

1978— Maybe there are other places in this land where the arrival of a front moving out of Canada can bring such a gasping sense of relief, but I doubt it can bring as much. The prospect is more hopeful even than the promise of rain after long drouth, though that too is blessed refreshment. But to know that the almost unending procession of days of one hundred degrees or more is about to come to a halt, that the thermals are even now being pushed south, that a touch of cool can be felt on the skin—it is like the sound of bagpipes to Lucknow, of the cavalry bugle to encircled wagons.

AUGUST 20

1956— At Springtown, in the shade of the principal business houses, the squatters hold session. Are they the only true

disciples of contemplation left? On the other hand, is their wisdom wasted? Squatting is not the easiest position known to man. To do it with dignity calls for a certain strength of mind as well as loin.

AUGUST 21

1944— Between Lubbock and Littlefield, as the sun went slowly down and the evening sky glowed a soft red, I saw a herd of rusty, fat Herefords plodding across a newly disked field of Permian soil, a study in reds, all somber tints, pastels, hues, shades.

AUGUST 22

1955— I can see from the long shadow of the oaks that summer is rapidly slanting, I almost say collapsing, into fall. One could draw up a ledger account, and thereby never regret that life gives way. What was alive, that hurt us or stung us into action or soothed us by its power to mystify, these made for enrichment. By what is taken away we measure how much was given.

AUGUST 23

1977— No man compares in mastery
with him who is in the saddle.

Nothing in modern imagery—climbing into a cock
    pit,
sliding on to the bench, seating oneself at the con
    sole—
none of these speaks of control
like extending the human bifurcation
over the spine of a horse.

AUGUST 24

1955— Near San Saba Peak, the road to the Colorado River led through desolate hills; the car scraped the cattleguards as we crossed. Rusty red rock, flat and jagged; agarita, cactus, mesquite, and many dead trees—practically no life except for a few cattle at one tank and an old bearded man sawing wood. In the river bottom we found an oasis, a great pecan under which we camped. On the path down to the river the smell of skunk lay heavy on one bush we passed. Datura, with moonlike flowers and long squashlike pods, bloomed. The river split upon a gravel bar and in one place a strong riffle sounded, though it became gentler the second day as the river dropped about three feet. Killdeer on the gravel bar cried and complained, sometimes as many as a dozen. At night the lambs and sheep called in the darkness. They and the mosquitoes kept me awake, but I enjoyed a night of stars such

as I have not seen in years. The Pleiades came up; I found I could not only count seven with a fair degree of ease, but sometimes an eighth or even more.

AUGUST 25
1978— When we stopped in Crowell the air seemed cool in the shade, but a truckload of steers parked on the county square bawled miserably, no doubt from thirst and heat. The wind was so strong at Copper Breaks State Park that I saw an ant making its way across the concrete platform of our shelter abruptly blown off. Other ants attempted to struggle off with crumbs of bread, and they too were buffeted back and forth. Through the glasses I saw a covey of quail gathered in the shade of a juniper, but I could not tell whether they were bobwhites or scaled. Saw two Mississippi kites over the breaks, saw doves, mockingbirds, heard a kingfisher at the pond. Copper Breaks gets its name from a small mining operation once conducted here. The wigwamlike shelters are unique and provide good protection. Although it was a very hot day, we were reasonably comfortable.

AUGUST 26
1956— Early in the day outside Gatesville I saw what I first

thought was a school bus in trouble, stopped at the side of the road as though someone had been run over. But it was a caravan of Mexican cotton pickers: the men were lying under the bus in its shade. Farther down the road women and small children sat in the shade of a live oak clump. Two jalopies had stopped at a distance behind the bus. This is not the first time I have seen migrants stop before noon, in the heat of the day, to cool off. They drive during the night so they will not overheat their motors or their passengers.

AUGUST 27

1973— It was not far to Missoula. I kept telling Mary that I'd bet nobody in the town had ever heard of Augustus Miles, the bass player ("There was once lived a man in the town of Missoula, His name was Augustus Miles; He was known miles around as a lallapaloosa, At playing the big bass viol.") Sure enough, I asked two persons; one of them seemed to think he had heard something like that once.

AUGUST 28

1975— Picking the black-eyed peas and thinking of the millions who do not even know these delightful vegetables exist. Making decisions whether a pod is sufficiently pregnant

or should be allowed to come nearer to term. Paying respect to bumblebees who are also feeding upon this delicious crop. I hardly realize that thought processes go on in my head.

AUGUST 29

1974— The heat of a Texas summer puts off my rambling.
Along with that, my mind has stopped working.
I'm an old horseshoe crab
who has to walk in order to chew.
I need exercise if I am to think.

AUGUST 30

1953— Galveston: Blue as a crab's leg. The fisherman casting his circular net, first catching the middle of it in his teeth as he makes ready to throw with both hands. The stately flight of pelicans, in tandem, and in almost perfect formation. Angel fish—"piggies"—grunting when caught; bluefish swelling. The fish market supplied by boats tied at the rear of each store: sheepshead, grouper, red snapper, mackerel, Jewfish, trout. Sulphur loading docks, utilizing endless belts. The sand eating out beneath our feet as we stand in the surf. The feeling of being pushed ashore by the waves when we lie down in the water.

AUGUST 31

1983— After the two-plus inches of rain that followed Hurricane Alicia's clouds, suddenly in our lawn rain lilies sprang up. I do not know how they do it, but I carefully counted them one evening, and the next morning several new ones had come up five to six inches tall. On the North Side I saw two large patches of them, containing each around a hundred flowers in an area no more than thirty square feet.

SEPTEMBER

SEPTEMBER 1

1978— North Rim of Grand Canyon. At Jacobs Lake we were told the North Rim would probably be full by the time we reached it. How about De Mott's Campground? We could probably camp there, so we proceeded and by luck found one spacious campsite left—enough really for three cars. When we occupied this primitive site about 4 P.M. it soon became evident that cars would be circling through the campgrounds much of the night. I told Mary it was a shame for us to occupy so large an area, and she agreed. I stopped a car which had made an unsuccessful search and offered to share the area. And thus we came to meet Claude and Thelma Allison, of Vinta, Oklahoma. He was, he said, self-employed, ran a few head of cattle on a farm and worked as an electrician part time.

Some of Claude Allison's stories: He had a horse which wasn't exactly broken, and tried to get it to cross a draw, but the horse didn't want to go at that particular point and began pitching. It threw him eventually and he landed on his face, but got up and got on the horse again and rode it. Mary mentioned the fact that she has never lived more than one mile from the place where she was born; he smiled and said, "Well, if you don't tell anybody about it it won't show." He didn't

particularly like horses, as some men do. He had to have them in his work, but he never was one to spend time grooming them and talking about them as a lot of fellows do. I asked him what kind of cow he preferred, after he spoke of the disadvantages of Charolais (calves too big to be born easily) and Limousin, and of Herefords, which get cancer-eye. Well, he didn't have any special favorite. It came down to whichever breed or hybrid would put on the most meat.

SEPTEMBER 2

1969— Old men sat at the bus stop in the center of town on a Saturday morning. I don't think they were waiting for a bus. They were waiting for Death, but here in the bustle of people they hoped they had found a safe place.

SEPTEMBER 3

1981— This morning while working in the garden as a drizzle fell, I noticed June bugs sticking in the tops of the Jerusalem artichokes. They seemed sleepy, lethargic, and I conceived the notion of tapping them into a container. I found a plastic milk jug and in fairly short time trapped a good number of them. Inside the jug they scrambled madly, but I could not tell whether some of their activity was from sexual frenzy.

Well, what should I do with a jugful of June bugs? I decided the easiest and most humane thing would be drown them, so I filled the jug with water. They floated to the top, and I could not help feeling more of a monster than a guardian of next year's roots.

SEPTEMBER 4

1960— We waited for the satellite but it didn't show up. I saw Antares and Jupiter, so why should I feel disappointed? Should a man choose between the intuition that comes in a flash and the light that burns there always in its season?

SEPTEMBER 5

1956— The sense of the ancient sea that once covered the earth here in Central Texas. I move like a snail upon an old seabed, and the headlands look down at every side.

SEPTEMBER 6

1977— The migration of birds
resembles Pickett's Charge. Thousands are lost
in frontal collisions with skyscrapers,
are picked off by rough predators,
buffeted by wind and storm.

But they keep coming on, advancing,
year after year, as if there were
no Cemetery Ridge.

SEPTEMBER 7

1980— The Great Beetle Battle: When I went out to bury
scraps in the compost pile I saw the garden had been taken
over by innumerable squadrons of—wasps, I thought first,
then saw they were June bugs. From digging experience I
knew their grubs have homesteaded my garden, and I said to
myself, I can at least decrease their numbers. Besides, it would
be great fun smashing them in midair. I found a rectangle of
wood and began laying about, even as that other left-hander,
John McEnroe, who so successfully defended his crown at
Flushing Meadow last Sunday. The board did little good; I
could not hit solidly with it. More than once I hit the collard
plants, to which the beetles seemed drawn. I saw, too, that
they were coming out of the soil, which yesterday's rain must
have given signal for a mighty emergence. Here and there
they were clustered in copulation and paid little heed when I
stepped on them. Which did little good—it pushed them into
the soft earth and out they came, clawing and clambering and
unhurt.

I thought of the badminton set in the garage and soon I was hacking about with a proper stroke. An occasional good forehand, a rare overhead smash, and I sent beetles flying. They came at me from all angles, maneuverable as Japanese Zeroes, and I carried the battle until my forearm grew too sore. At the end there were as many as ever. I retired from the field, a combination Mitty-McEnroe, having missed far more shots than I ever hit, content, nevertheless, I at least had met the enemy.

SEPTEMBER 8

1965— At Indiana Dunes boys and girls played up and down the dunes, making tracks down the slopes on which they rolled tin cans. During the night four coons visited the garbage basket near our camp. When they waked me with their grunting and snarling I could think only of a porcupine. When I shined the flashlight into their eyes all but one backed away into the darkness: this one ignored me. Strangely, next morning there was a dead coon just outside a nearby camp, no sign of what had killed it.

SEPTEMBER 9

1967— The sight of shorebirds on a mudflat
      brings something like nostalgia, though it stems

from the opposite of causes.
Absence of home or province marks them.
Casting themselves across two continents,
they tempt us to be sorry for them.
Not to say, though, when they pass
together in precision, circle, and depart,
"Sic transit gloria." No need.
They own the whole world.

SEPTEMBER 10

1984— The barber pointed to a Mr. J_____ just leaving the
shop. Said he had a way of naming the hairs on his head.
"Cut Buford a little but leave George alone," he would say.
And yet he has a fair share of hair. For a while it seems he
had worn a "wig" (as the barber called it), but when he dis-
continued this, it could be seen he was by no means bald.

SEPTEMBER 11

1974— The delicate yellow blooms of broomweed—
I find them beside sidewalks in the central city.
There's a whole botany to be discovered
in the cracks, on the curbs, over broken concrete.
A weed doesn't care if it grows
in the rubble of a city.

SEPTEMBER 12

1974— My youngest taught me I had a rare distinction: simian lines in both hands, long unbroken creases the width of the palm. I never found much use for them until today, when pouring turnip seed (which is devilishly small) back into a vial. That neat little furrow of flesh! A perfect sluice to play the seed into safekeeping.

SEPTEMBER 13

1977— This morning in the clumped grass south of the gully in the river bottom, I again flushed the family of quail. They were there yesterday. To my startled eye they appeared just fledged enough to fly, the mother about twice their size. She flew to a chinaberry where I could hear her calling plaintively. Whether they find in this spot some special grass seed to lunch on, or whether this is their nightly roosting place I cannot tell. I searched through the grass for the telltale ring of droppings that marks a night's bivouac, but found none.

SEPTEMBER 14

1974— When we look up at night it is not the dark
      we fix on, but rather the stars.
      Valery's saying the nothingness shows through
      in God's Creation tells but half.

It is even truer to say
that in the emptiness of Chaos
Something is awake.

SEPTEMBER 15

1957— At San Saba the postmaster told me the townspeople
customarily go out to the river when a rise is coming down,
because there is something in the water out of the alkali hills
that stuns fish. They come to the top and can be taken by
hand. Or if the rise is mild, you can feel for them just under
the surface. On the Colorado River it is even worse; sometimes the fish die.

SEPTEMBER 16

1973— During the night—
     do I imagine it is only at night?—
     while all the rest of the city is still,
     they bring forth the great brute jets at Carswell
     and subject them to torture.
     They bellow as no living, mortal creatures
     ever dreamed of bellowing,
     and yet they give a sense of a titanic suffering
     in something that lives, if only a saurian body.

In the darkness I feel them shudder against the ground
as they open their obscene torches to hiss,
to shriek, to roar upon the men that goad them.
Why this is done I do not know.
Some strange function of the Air Force, no doubt,
to assure the world all is secure
so long as these dragons stand guard.

SEPTEMBER 17

1976— I gathered some mesquite beans at the state park in Abilene and took pains to dry them before I tried to grind them. They didn't grind well: the pulp was still a little syrupy, and the thin seeds had a way of slipping through the handmill whole no matter how I adjusted it. Mary fixed pancakes this morning with a fourth-cup of mesquite flour in the batter. It is almost noon and I have had no ill effects. There was a wild, strong taste, a good one, in those cakes. Clinically, I did notice later a seed or two managed to slip through not only the grinder but me as well, whole and entire.

SEPTEMBER 18

1971— West of Mineral Wells we went horseback riding over a trail that led through mesquite and rock, down a path

made up of cracked limestone that could not have been more treacherous. The horses at times stopped to consider whether it was safe to take another step; then, falling behind, they would dash recklessly down the trail to catch up with the rest of the train. It is an eerie feeling when the front of a horse dips down off one ledge to another, but we let the beasts do their own navigating and somehow came out safely.

SEPTEMBER 19

1973— How satisfying it must be
for that butterfly to lay eggs on my collard leaf
that look like, magnified, Christmas tree globes.
And to rack them up in little clumps
like celestial billiard balls!

SEPTEMBER 20

1965— At evening, an enormous white rose of thunderhead at the zenith, with one small blushing patch of pink. It vibrated with sheet lightning. I never saw a rose whose waxen skin winked, quivered so. Occasionally hairpins of lightning broke around it.

SEPTEMBER 21

1959— The mimosa is wearing epaulets these days. When I came outdoors, a startled mockingbird rustled the pods as it took off from the tree.

SEPTEMBER 22

1974— I almost always give the poor blind woman
    who sings hymns on the corner a quarter or so.
    Still, I know it isn't primarily
    out of charitable impulse, either.
    It is my penance for having once suggested
    to my boys: I planned to give her a dollar
    if she would only stop singing
    until I was out of hearing.

SEPTEMBER 23

1974— One of the wettest of Septembers ever.
    The cedar elms are heavy with disks,
    the grass is studded with mangy toadstools.
    Great droves of cotton rats
    have swarmed in from the soggy fields.
    The sun has sliced through the overcast
    only a few times
    and then pulled hastily back.

SEPTEMBER 24

1976— Snowstorms having been preempted
(and none too available in this region)
there's no position open, unless
one wants to be plenipotentiary
to the weeds.

SEPTEMBER 25

1974— A couple of ruby-throated hummingbirds are fre-
quenting our back yard: the red Turk's-cap and the bean blossoms give them a little food, I suppose. Most often, though, I
see them sitting hunched on the utility wire that passes over
our pyracantha, looking (it seems to me) pretty miserable.

SEPTEMBER 26

1973— If a man must know himself, the first thing he must
do is set about knowing who he is not. Whence arises the
need for specificity. I am not that butterfly flying in my garden. Which butterfly? The blue-green with red dashes on its
upper wings. You know, the red-spotted purple—*Limenitis
astyanax.*

SEPTEMBER 27

1971— The mind is a great Wanderer,
      and it is a crime to attach it to traces,
      to set it plowing in one field.
      It was meant to soar like the vulture,
      to bound like the dik-dik,
      range over rough terrain like a bison.
      We fence it like some draft horse
      and then wonder it grows mean of spirit.

SEPTEMBER 28

1980— I am sitting in the car at a shopping center, waiting for Mary to return. It is still raining: a steady rain, not a drizzle, yet neither a downpour. The drops strike the windshield and slowly slide down the inclined plane. I cannot figure out why so slowly—they move almost glacially. There must be an attraction, a surface tension set up when the drops strike the glass, not enough to hold the drops fast, but enough to catch them and restrain their descent.

SEPTEMBER 29
1951— Downtown: A truckload of braceros, fitted with a tarpaulin to shade the brood of children of all ages who stood staring out at the city. I was almost run over by an ancient car that followed the truck, the occupants running through a red light with a sort of wild look.

SEPTEMBER 30
1971— We are on the brink of October,
         poised to fall into golden days
         like leaves turned crisp before frost.
         The air is the best of the temperate zone:
         it will move, it will cool and exhilarate.
         This is the best month of the year:
         here in Texas the winter to come
         does not loom up behind it, casting a shadow.
         October blesses, because hot summer is over,
         because the resident birds of winter return,
         because the fields are yellow
         with broomweed and daisy.

OCTOBER

OCTOBER 1

1975— The time comes when the day must be unclutched.
The moment we first seized hold,
a notice to disengage began.

OCTOBER 2

1976— In the Trinity channel next to the old dike road, a long string of whirligigs, about fifteen feet by six inches, huddled quietly by the bank, not moving. Do they numbly apprehend the coming winter?

OCTOBER 3

1975— When a man no longer has the fury of youth
he can no longer risk throwing
the perfect strike.
He must aim for the outside corner,
put some kind of twist on his words,
or even throw a few bad pitches
hoping the reader cannot resist.

OCTOBER 4

1976— Somewhere I lost a whole tree, a basswood that stood on the south side of the river bottom gully. I discovered it with a good deal of pride, with its odd little fruit seeming to

come out of the middle of an ill-shaped leaf. This spring I looked and waited patiently to find it in bloom—bees, they say, are greatly attracted. But it never made an appearance and I cannot locate it. I fear some Park Department employee, eager to tame the wild edges, bulldozed it down.

OCTOBER 5

1973— At the dude ranch west of Mineral Wells, where our Presbyterian choir had gone for a retreat, twice during the night a canyon wren broke into song. That swooning, hysterical, downward chromatic—haven't I heard it before, in the Tempest Etude of Chopin?

OCTOBER 6

1971— For years I lived under the mistaken notion
　　　　that winter is when the birds fly south.
　　　　So they do. But here in Texas
　　　　more come down from the north
　　　　than depart farther south.
　　　　On occasion I have dimly understood
　　　　the same exchange operates in my life:
　　　　even while I bemoan a loss
　　　　a tide of beneficence sweeps in.

OCTOBER 7

1967— I'd a lot rather be a pecan, give up my fruit all at once in a shower of nuggets. Let them fall into the clutter, the rich mold, to give pleasure perhaps to someone who loves to scratch among leaves. Or let them sink into soil and father saplings.

OCTOBER 8

1978— At the Oktoberfest I had to take tickets and stamp the backs of hands with a rubber stamp. I learned a great deal about the human hand. For one thing, there are great differences of texture, boniness, plumpness or leanness: on some I almost feared to press the stamp, thinking it might break a bone. Others had a firm embonpoint, inviting a stout impression. But I learned even more about the character of Texans. Some did not know I was going to stamp them: when I seized a hand the reaction was without fail friendly. Several thought I was shaking the hand as a greeter, and they responded warmly. None of the ladies drew back, unless to point to tickets held by their male companions. Some of them even fluttered a little, and one said, "I only just got here and somebody is already holding my hand."

OCTOBER 9

1954— A squadron of scissortails in the mesquite pasture west of Carter Field. They all sit on barbed wire or mesquite branches, all with shining breasts to the sun, but when they fly, the beautiful salmon beneath their wings is exposed. At this time of year they are gathering for migration, and the sound of a small flock sputtering to itself is strangely like a little gasoline engine missing fire.

OCTOBER 10

1978— At certain seasons we used to say "Lake Worth is turning over," because the water from the kitchen faucet tasted funny. It seems to me I remember past years—the sixties, for instance—when history tasted funny. Many things were turning over.

OCTOBER 11

1974— The mockingbird's song in October
      differs in quality from his spring outpouring—
      more tentative, quizzical, less rapturous,
      as though over summer he had turned
      from romantic into classicist.
      Not so much that the fires had died down

or technique been forgotten
as that experience has urged on him
the strategic value of restraint.

OCTOBER 12

1971— I hear the whining of a truck changing gears on Interstate 35 and the shrieking of a blue jay in the woods between. In the ecology of the twenty-first century I hope a place for both will remain. If we elaborate new species of machine, let them tune to the existence of living creatures.

OCTOBER 13

1973— With unaccountable joy I read
(and I go immediately to the yard to confirm)
that the hackberry leaf is three-ribbed.
And so this one is,
though I must turn it upside down to test it.
I know why it pleases: out there in amorphous space
another being has nailed down a form.
Of one thing I increase in awareness:
it is Life that evidences Order.
The inorganic may be a great spread of atoms
but whatever Life is, it is shape,

structure that satisfies our immortal craving
for design. For this alone we can give reverence.

OCTOBER 14

1964— This the strawberry month—not the fruit, but the tint.
Everywhere the grasses are rusting into bright strawberry
tones. Awns, stems, foliage brighten the ground.

OCTOBER 15

1945— In the peanut counties to the southwest of us long
rains have spoiled the curing hay and started many of the
nuts to sprouting, even those underground. Tractors sit in the
fields, hunched, with small forepaws and great haunches,
huge, ungainly metal rabbits cowering in the rain.

OCTOBER 16

1978— I always look forward to October:
    to going out in the yard
    and watching the grass slow down.

OCTOBER 17

1977— The custodian at First Presbyterian said that when
they opened the doors on a Sunday morning the candle flies

were so thick he didn't know if they could hold church. Candle flies? I never heard the term, even though it sounded ecclesiastical. And then I understood: the little moths or skippers that are everywhere these days, by the thousands. But I do like his name for them.

OCTOBER 18

1976— As I go out to get the morning paper
a sound of the seasons greets me—
the crunch of dead leaves underfoot on the sidewalk.
Last night the first norther of the year came through:
today the elm leaves are almost down.

OCTOBER 19

1961— At the Dallas Fair the hogs were being given cholera shots. One man slipped a metal loop (at the end of a stick) around the snout and under the top jaw, the other went behind and slapped the beast on the ham. Each hog so treated invariably tensed its ham, and then the needle was stuck in. All this while the victim stood screaming one long high-pitched squeal. Over in another pen a duroc sow stood and one pig punched furiously at her teats without making much connection. Then she lay down and almost as one the other pigs, eight or nine of them, rose and attacked her wallowing

belly—vigorously until the whole rose and fell like waves breaking in crests against a seawall.

OCTOBER 20

1974— The State of the Road this day: The asters are in bloom; frostweed is dead or dying; the leaves of the Mexican buckeye are gone, laying bare the pawnshop balls of the seed capsules; the green ash is turning red at its tips; many red berries spangle the haws. At the edge of the abandoned stable an elderly black man is forking the ground, but he is not taking manure, as I did. What is he doing? He is digging for worms to go fishing.

OCTOBER 21

1969— Our world exists tonight
      in the beat of the cricket:
      like a hasty sea of sound coming in
      on the shore of consciousness,
      faster than any waves on a beach
      yet in the same unceasing rhythm.

OCTOBER 22

1975— Like any good Texan,
      all that I ask

is an allowance
for being depleted.

OCTOBER 23

1975— This is that hour of the day, that time of the year,
when the sun strikes the glass windows of the downtown skyscrapers until, as I look southwestward across the Trinity,
they burst into fire. Did people build these structures, a modern Stonehenge, just so that once a year the light makes a
revelation?

OCTOBER 24

1971— A small lizard inhabits the floor of our garage these
days. I squatted to examine him and he stared back at me
fearlessly. He held his tail stiffly in an upward curve off the
floor, to show, no doubt, how long he could sustain the trick.
A couple of times he did a quick push-up. Once he darted
toward me and caught and swallowed a lesser insect, possibly an ant. His four-clawed feet had such fine slender toes I
wondered they did not fray away or snap off.

OCTOBER 25

1978— I went down on a drizzly morning determined to open

the red berries of the Carolina moonseed that I found in an angle of two streets, for the sole purpose of seeing whether the seeds really do resemble (as the textbooks say) the crescent moon. The first I tried was wholly round, the second a little less so, and the third and fourth more gibbous than crescent. You'd need the state of mind that comes with a full moon to make crescents out of them. Going back up Dalford Hill I plucked the small fruit of a sugar hackberry and nipped off the pulp, looked at the seed. Now *there* was a moon— almost perfectly round and golden as a harvest pumpkin coming swollen over the horizon.

OCTOBER 26

1976— Here on our small bluff looking southeast to the city we have survived four great stenches since I came as a boy to this part of the world. We came at the beginning of winter and quickly got acquainted with the first, the putrid smell of offal and dung sweeping over the town from the Swift and Armour plants on the North Side. Every norther brought a fresh flood. There were also days when the refineries due north of us let off a chemical miasma that made us wonder if we dared strike a match in the open air. In the summer when the Trinity sank low and the Gulf breeze blew out of the south,

the stink of the river blended with the vileness of the sewage disposal plant in East Riverside. Then on summer evenings the city dump on Cold Springs Road would blanket the whole area with thick, nauseous smoke. Strange. All these are gone. Swift and Armour are largely demolished. The refineries are diminished or almost disappeared. The sewage disposal plant is moving farther east. The burning of refuse is no longer permitted. The air is clean except for the noise and fumes from the interstate highway that make their presence known night and day. The old disorder passes, to make way for the new.

OCTOBER 27
1976— The year dies, and the squirrel and bird nests begin to appear in the trees as the leaves depart. The heads of pigweed turn dark purple or bright red. The midrib of the curly dock is also scarlet, as is an occasional leaf. The little leather flower has on it a fruit similar to the sweetgum's. Sawleaf daisies are dried and brown, their heads masses of ecru spheres. The prickly poppies are loaded with burs. I started up a large covey of quail feeding in the sunflowers on the riverbank. Our winter resident red-tailed hawk has returned to patrol the river.

OCTOBER 28

1978— A committee of sparrows
has landed on the air conditioner outside:
they seem to be engaged
in a procedural brawl—
trying to elect a suitable chirp-person.

OCTOBER 29

1957— At Chalk Mountain a long band of sumac at the foot
of the hills, vivid red below the dark green of the cedar. I
have never seen sumac more strikingly colored: there are all
tones of copper, copper fresh from the smelter, copper with a
heavy patina. The outer leaves and outer tips turn first and
are the most brilliant in a bush newly touched by frost. These
shrubs have the appearance of sponges, green sponges being
eaten by a weather that turns them gradually lifeless and
brown.

OCTOBER 30

1974— The white-throated sparrow comes again for winter;
we wouldn't know if it were not
for that poignant little piccolo,
almost lost in the orchestration of a city.

"Like having your children come home,"
said Mary, when out in the backyard
the first one of the season called.

OCTOBER 31

1976— Tonight I will pull the plugs of all the clocks
and let them rest in the dark while the world turns
from Daylight Saving back to Standard Time.
Now that I think of it, Death too is only
a pulling of the plug to let
Eternity catch up.

NOVEMBER

NOVEMBER 1

1971— Caterpillars
and other adolescents
never die of old age.
Sometimes, though,
of transfiguration.

NOVEMBER 2

1979— As I mow the grass in my heavy shoes, from time to time I feel a round lump concealed in the turf, and stooping, find a fallen pecan. I can't help wondering how a nut can burrow out of sight of man and squirrel and blue jay so easily. Still, my being able to detect it with the sole of my shod foot puts me in a class with those butterflies that taste the ripeness of flowers merely by walking on them. Who knows, with a little more effort, what metamorphosis I might aspire to?

NOVEMBER 3

1963— Mary and I spent almost two hours on the island off Lakeshore Drive, and we penetrated the deepest thicket hoping to slip upon some wary ducks. We found great riches: a magnificent mulberry tree, which is surely the delight of all

manner of birds in the fruiting season; a splendid mass of brown fungus, like a volcanic heap of scrambled eggs; holly bushes in red berry; rotting logs and hollow trees from which skunks and other animals had lately departed. Red-bellied woodpeckers and flickers came about us fearlessly. We sat in the middle of a sand road while kinglets and chickadees and titmice busied themselves in the branches above us. The kinglets especially, little hunchbacks with great eyes, clambering among chandeliers.

NOVEMBER 4

1974— A cold day today: tonight perhaps the first freeze
of winter. The green ash has taken on color,
the center of the tree yet green, the outer leaves
touched with yellow, here and there some turned
deep red. The chinaberries almost rival aspens
in the tenderness of solid yellow.
I saw a grapevine on which leaves hung
in utter aspect of decay—great rusty holes
and tawny notches fallen out.
I walked down to the river, which is in flood:
a boy's body, they say, is still in that torrent.

NOVEMBER 5

1978— There is a diminished quality in the afternoon light
as I come out for a walk this day. Not a cloud in the sky and
the sun at full power, yet with a certain languor and tenta-
tiveness. Perhaps we are more sensitive to the changing light
than we know—as much so as the leaves except only that we
do not know how to make starch.

NOVEMBER 6

1974— On the Refuge an expert identified for us some of
the native grasses. One was sideoats grama. He pointed to
the spikelets that come out of the stem at different degrees
around it, but all turn—some as much as 180 degrees—in
order to stand in the same plane as the others. Now what makes
this desirable? (There must be a purpose: does it facilitate
pollination?) Surely it does not do this simply to provide my
eye with an appreciation of sideoatery.

NOVEMBER 7

1975— On my morning walk to the river bottom I occasionally arrive ahead of the fat lady and her companion who are
apparently determined to make a sweep of the pecan crop
before the riffraff come and steal their rightful gains from

them. It is a public park now; anyone can go nutting. I have pecans of my own but I cannot resist scrutinizing and scratching to see what the night winds have brought down. Sometimes the ground is rich with nuggets. I begin to distinguish between one-nut and two- (or even more) nut stoops. It is pleasant while doing this to hear the plop of a brown shell hitting the soil, reminding me that the tree has not yet done with delivering. I even imagine that, according to the direction of the wind last night, the fall is more bountiful on this side of the tree or that. If I could rid myself of the feeling of guilt at taking what others want so badly (I can almost feel the stares of the fat lady and her friend burn into my back), I could leave joyfully. As it is, I climb Dalford Hill with my pockets stuffed like a gopher's cheeks, so full, pecans pop out with each step I take, and I know what it is to be one of the Haves in a world of Have-nots.

NOVEMBER 8

1975— Part of the pull of religious faith lies in the difficulty of sustaining it. If it were easy to come by and keep sturdy, who would place much value in it? I thought this as we sat, a group of bass singers, trying with the aid of a noble bassoon to learn the melismas of the Magnificat. Why, I wondered,

did Bach make his sacred music so devilishly difficult? Was it not to entice the doubters, the waverers, the semi-competent? If you can learn to sing these lines, he says across the centuries, you can even learn to believe.

NOVEMBER 9

1970— Out of Winnsboro we stopped at a small shop on the autumn trail and there we talked with the proprietor. I asked about the squashes they had displayed for sale in an earlier year. "The cushawls?" he asked. He'd raised them for two years but it seemed like they didn't go very well. The striped ones had the best flavor. He'd had a good grape crop this year, but in August it rained so much the grapes swelled and began to drop off. He was thin and wiry, a little drawn in the face, wore a straw hat with double-curled brim, and he repeatedly said "cushawls," but I took him for the salt of the earth.

NOVEMBER 10

1968— I sat in church by a Rustling Rembrandt,
a child who with his pencil and paper
made worship a mockery for me.

I wanted to snatch his pencil out of his hands and
    break it.
I can feel old Elisha under my skin.

NOVEMBER 11
1974— At sundown at the Nature Center the sky was still
watery-bright when wedge and line after wedge and line of
Franklin's gulls came out of the south, far up in that crisp air.
At first we could not guess what they were: no usual book I
ever read speaks of their flying in V's and lines like this, but
Bent's life histories do. In this south-flying time, where had
they been, where were they going? It was fast darkening and
they would soon need to settle.

NOVEMBER 12
1961— The fellow in the restaurant in Washington, a chief
of communications and expert on radiation (it appeared). He
was telling his companions of a song a group had made up, to
the tune of "The Streets of Laredo." "Our headgears were
crackling like grease in the pan, I wrote my wife, Dear Friend,
it began, and ended, Poor widow, go find a new man." He
also told of throwing a big party in Japan. He spoke of open-

ing a bottle of Manischewitz and inviting anyone who wanted to become a convert to drink. At the same time he took out his knife and began whetting it. "They knew I'd use it, too." He was an articulate fellow. He quoted Browning, "Or what's a heaven for?" He spoke of his wife, who played Beethoven and Mozart, and would be most happy if she hadn't married him.

NOVEMBER 13

1971— When the wind gusts through the cottonwood
　　　 I cannot hear the individual leaves clatter.
　　　 But as it begins to rise or it dies away,
　　　 I detect them,
　　　 a scattered, leathery applause.

NOVEMBER 14

1973— As we lolled in the backyard, I complained to Susan about the leaves falling on our lawn. Would she help me glue them back on the redbud? Now she is only five years old and she knew this was silly, but grandpas have to be humored. When I went into the house and got the glue, she tried valiantly to make a leaf or two stick to a twig, but they would not. Then we sat in the swing in resignation and watched the

stream of dead foliage, great heart-shaped ghosts, continue to fall.

NOVEMBER 15
1974— In the cracks of the sidewalks downtown
the lowly prostrate spurge begins to turn
alizarin red.

NOVEMBER 16
1972— Perhaps this is what it is to grow old: to think magnificent thoughts, marvelously ingenious thoughts in a kind of somnambulistic haze, and then to realize with a start that the vision has come and gone, that you are not able to summon it back into the arena of the conscious mind. To know grace and adventure so close at hand but to apprehend them only as long-forgotten joys.

NOVEMBER 17
1973— This season I will give thanks
for a most unexpected gift:
that I have been given time to begin to know
my friends and neighbors—the Trees,
the Grasses, the Flowers, the Weeds.

NOVEMBER 18

1975— A man prefers to think of himself
as a mountain range, a grand valley, a noble forest;
but nearing his last years he knows
himself to be more like a swamp.
Which is not so bad:
where is life richer than in a good swamp?
There need be nothing dismal about the place—
where are more singing birds
or chorusing frogs
or flapping fish?

NOVEMBER 19

1971— The trees have their own individuality. Our elm has
lost most of its leaves, while those down the street are only
now in full yellow. The cottonwood is untouched green, while
across the drive a pecan passes beyond gold. They each drink
a different draft of chemicals from the subsoil, and they stand
in different places regarding the sun, the wind, the soil, the
slope. Like poor artists, we should have colored them all the
same had their turning been left to us. But chance and character have intervened.

NOVEMBER 20

1975— Nothing contributes to the pleasure
of a morning's walk so much
as a certain soreness in the bones.

NOVEMBER 21

1973— Human creatures are so constructed they cannot read while walking vigorously. Count this a great fortune, for otherwise many might be tempted to feed their minds into the hoppers of books instead of turning the marvelous world before their eyes into the sieve of thought. Still, there is no need to hurry: the only reason for walking faster than you want to is that you are unable to run. I can imagine no absolute need for walking at forced draft unless it be that a porpoise is treading on your tail. For God's sake, let your poor body set its own pace.

NOVEMBER 22

1963— I went out before noon, to do some Christmas shopping in the Dallas stores and let others in my office go later so that they could see him. No one could walk through the streets without feeling an uneasiness in the air. I saw a traffic

patrolman taking off his yellow raingear; the sun was breaking through clouds. Later, back in my office, I heard the carillon in the Mercantile Bank playing "Hail to the Chief." And shortly thereafter it turned suddenly to "What a Friend We Have in Jesus." "What in the world are they playing that for?" I asked a secretary. Abruptly, an engineer came to my door. "Can you stand a shock?" he asked. Sure. "The President has been shot!"

NOVEMBER 23

1969— Part of the pleasure of a windy night
　　　　comes from the randomness of the squeaks
　　　　and rattles of an old house.
　　　　They follow no rhythm in particular.
　　　　Wakeful, I listen and think I detect
　　　　a presence, not necessarily evil,
　　　　but Something there in the darkness,
　　　　in the attic, on the stair, going about
　　　　its own peculiar business.

NOVEMBER 24

1973— While I sat in the choir the thought came to me:
　　　　Satan appears to Christ in the Wilderness.

"Your name," he says, "has been chosen
as one of the leading Prophets of our time.
We want to include your biography
in our new directory, *These Are Those*.
But you must hurry. Our offer closes this month."
And then he mentions offhandedly,
"It will only cost you fifty dollars
to have your very own copy."

NOVEMBER 25

1977— In the state park at Tyler we gathered sassafras
leaves, yellow and orange and reddish, all of the three-lobed
kind. I laid them out on the ground and cement in a trail leading into our shelter. They looked much like the three-toed
dinosaur tracks we see at Glen Rose in the Paluxy River. All
this, for what? So Mary could take a picture, and I would be
able to show our granddaughters the spoor of the horrible
Sassafras Monster.

NOVEMBER 26

1974— The starlings are imitating meadowlarks—
         ineptly, weakly, but no doubt about it,
         aping their yellow-breasted cousins.

More often than not, they give a little jeery
whistle afterward, as if to say,
"So, we are not very good imitators,
what then?"

NOVEMBER 27

1976— A windy, cold day. I remember
our basil seed needs separating.
What better than to winnow it?
But I soon find out there's more to the job
than thinking about it. You have to take care
gusts do not carry away both chaff and seed.
And in taking care you grow too careful,
do not give freedom to the wind.
In winnowing, as in all crafts,
a great part of art is letting go.

NOVEMBER 28

1977— The thought struck me with peculiar force as I was
out walking: there is nobody I would rather be. The notion
seems overweening, if not downright sinful, but it's really
harmless. Seeing I cannot know what fears and failures plague

the inner workings of other men, it is only reasonable I prefer to take chances with my own makeup, however lacking. Doesn't every man, woman, or child think him- or herself the supreme Act of Creation, give or take a few flaws here and there?

NOVEMBER 29

1954— I ride these days between Dallas and Fort Worth in a world of two colors, red and black. The land is a stygian plain stretching undifferentiated except for the iron tracery of trees, bare of leaves, against a dull glowing stratum of red where the sun has just gone down. Tonight a long trail of smoke hangs penciled across the horizon. But the blackest part of all on a winter night is not the night but the earth itself, shorn of illumination. In comparison, the sky is friendly.

NOVEMBER 30

1979— On the last day of November the summer's leaves
resign in a body. The mulberries let go in masses
till the street is almost covered. I work an hour
gathering up under just three trees.
Sometimes I stop to see how it is

with the pecans and the cottonwood: a few leaves
hang in their branches, but never a minute passes
one does not suddenly let go and fall to the ground.
How to describe that descent? There is a hopeless-
    ness,
withal a dignity, in the detachment.
No shriek accompanies the tearing
of the abscission layer. So does the body of a man
    or woman
forsake the human race. It was in seeing a leaf de-
    scend
so slowly to the earth that the first theologian
spoke of the flesh returning to dust.

DECEMBER

DECEMBER 1

1943— In the desolate little town of Swearingen I met Postmaster George Washington Hare. There is nothing to the town now, that once had several hotels, except the old building housing the post office and a large room crammed with his library of pharmacopoeia and other books. He showed me a first edition volume, signed by some famous author, Bulwer-Lytton, if I remember aright. While we talked a straggle of mules came wandering into his yard, and he ran out to berate them and shoo them away. This town is on a railroad that once was projected to reach the Pacific—the Quanah, Acme & Pacific, Q A & P. Now, he told me, people call it the "Quit Arguin' and Push."

DECEMBER 2

1962— During the night the moon has described an immense horseshoe, beginning in gold and ending in silver, enough to span a night's sleep.

DECEMBER 3

1977— Ted Brant and I stopped north of Glen Rose to look at the nuclear reactor going up in the distant hills to the west, and where we stopped I suddenly noticed insect bodies pinned

on the barbs of a fence paralleling the road. It was new wire, and we wondered: had the sharp metal encouraged shrikes to wholesale murder? We counted about a hundred victims, ranging from one small frog to grasshoppers, beetles, dragonflies, crickets, bees.

DECEMBER 4

1961— One way by which I have always known it is winter is by the huge bloom of steam billowing up from the electric plant on North Main, below Paddock Viaduct, the vapor condensing fiercely white in the new cold.

DECEMBER 5

1975— The poplar I planted years ago
        holds to its leaves amazingly long
        this season. A week ago the tree turned golden,
        a brilliance none other near knows,
        and yet it clung to its brood with fierceness.
        A touch of norther, a brief rain last night,
        and this morning the yard is carpeted
        with gold spatter. I am led to think
        each leaf knows how to turn its bright side up;
        but it isn't so—a closer look

shows many dull undersides to the air.
Still, there's some magic here:
how did the tree and the elements contrive
to scatter glitter so evenly?
If I painted this scene from memory
there'd be big clusters of gold and small patches
of gray for relief. But that's not what I see.
They are laid down like mosaic
as if to be sure the gold
goes as far as it can.

DECEMBER 6

1961— We went across from El Paso into Juarez to a small
restaurant where one of us knew the proprietor. "What is good
on the menu?" my friend asked. The proprietor shrugged and
took back the menus he had distributed. "The same old bull,"
he said. It was drizzling outside and newspapers were spotted on the floor strategically to catch drippings from the ceil-
ing. A string quartet, violin, viola, bass, guitar, played at intervals, not always true but recognizable. On the streets men
approached us constantly, offering to take us to "Erma's." A
taxicab driver told us about them. These men work for the
establishment. Juarez has about five thousand prostitutes, all

licensed by the State. They must pay $2.50 a day for the privilege of working. Twice a week they are given a health examination. They may not ply their trade on the street and may be sent to jail if caught doing so. They have a union and an organization representative. They have been known to go on strike and to ruin the owner of a house who has displeased them. Also on the streets, in tiny booths, were men selling puppets. Many times we saw the same puppet: a caricature of a Mexican peon, dancing in front of us.

DECEMBER 7
1952— The girl in the Shrine Circus Parade: In the lower end of the city I saw her mount her elephant howdah, dressed in blue jeans. They threw her veils up to her, and here she is, coming up Main Street, a veritable Arabian houri.

DECEMBER 8
1958— In Dallas a rough-looking woman in bobby socks and knitted cap stood in front of Green's Department Store, haranguing passersby. I assumed it was a religious message but could not distinguish her shouting, which had a curious bitterness to it.

DECEMBER 9

1975— One by one the cells of the brain
    wither and go to oblivion.
    Outside, trees are losing their leaves
    at a quickening pace.
    I have no buds to replace the dying cells;
    but the same winter symmetries of boughs
    again appear to comfort me.

DECEMBER 10

1977— On the highway east of Mineral Wells there is a deep
cut through the layered sandstone. The sandwiched stacks of
stone always catch my eye, and today I notice how exactly
their color matches that of the dead leaves on the post oaks at
either side.

DECEMBER 11

1957— As I drove past the dairy on the hills east of town,
momentarily I caught sight of the Fort Worth skyline, framed
under the udder of a cow.

DECEMBER 12

1954— The fog has suddenly become very heavy, but I can
still make out an occasional horse or cow munching the pale

new grass in roadside pastures. It causes me to wonder whether fresh grass with the taste of fog in it is not a delectable salad indeed.

DECEMBER 13

1980— At Fred's place on Possum Kingdom Lake we went for a walk, a whole troop of us, and on the way back Fred spotted a citron by the roadside. He picked it up and showed us how the thing would actually bounce if you threw it down. It was about the size of a football and that set off a game of tossing it. Someone threw it to me and it slipped through my hands and hit me in the mouth. Bruised my lip and my dignity, but I can now say without qualification that I have been bashed in the face with a flying watermelon. The citron also had a sandbur on it, and it made my left hand bleed. Fred says there were many of these in the fields when he first moved here. You have to make sure none grow near your watermelon patch, as they will cross and cause your tame melons to have extremely thick rinds.

DECEMBER 14

1974— A hard freeze last night and twenty-five degrees this morning, though quite sunny. I made my usual round on my walk and found a surprise at the bottom of Dalford Hill. The

frostweed had erupted on December 3, but that was only a minor outburst. This morning they had billowed out great cottony masses that shone in the sun like spun glass. A neighbor pointed out that the splitting of the stem went rather high on some of the plants—the "frost" showed almost a foot high on those on the hillside.

DECEMBER 15
1968— I decided to punish the world
         by withholding my talent.
         It was as if I stood in midwinter,
         the only blade of grass that still clung to
         its meager seed.
         Even the sparrows despised me.

DECEMBER 16
1956— On the bus I heard a fellow tell his companion, "They say it's the driest in seven hundred years in West Texas. How can they say that? They haven't had weather records that long."

DECEMBER 17
1971— Plant some of your hopes
         in the cold of winter:

there are singular joys that come to bloom
only if they have felt
the frigid tooth of December.

DECEMBER 18

1971— I believe the film
remains forever fresh.
It is only that dust and abrasion
becloud the lens.

DECEMBER 19

1976— There is one thing I do regret,
and that is not having taken
a closer look.

DECEMBER 20

1957— A wild and, in its violent way, a beautiful day. When I left San Angelo at noon a dust storm was reaching its height. It increased in fury and disclosed strange scenes: as I drove east to Veribest the pall of dust shrouded the mesquite with a weird white cast, much like fog. Still, I could see mistletoe and birds' nests in the branches. The highway led directly across the path of the wind, and from the north innumerable balls of tumbleweed came bounding and rolling across the

pavement. Their motion, a kind of lope, results from the fact
that they are seldom perfectly globular, but rather lobed and
ellipsoid; their motion reminded me of galloping cows, an-
gular and bony. Many were driven against fences to become
hopelessly lodged, even as cattle in blizzards are said to be.
East of Veribest the dust came so thick that at times I could
not see the road. I passed two huddled flocks of sheep, dirty-
brown with dust. The first flock gathered in a sort of dough-
nut or fungus ring. There is a strange fascination in a dust
storm, unless you have to live where they thrive. The mys-
tery and terror of the sky scourge the pretensions of the human mind so contemptuously the imagination cannot fail to
be impressed.

DECEMBER 21

1974— When I was a young man I seldom knew
        what I was talking about. But thank the Lord,
        I kept on talking and sometimes thinking
        until arrived at a time
        when I had a true glimmer.

DECEMBER 22

1976— It seems a bit foolish on the brink of a new year, to
think ahead to one a few posts farther down the road. But

why not now begin to shape our arrival into that famous year, 1984, so as to belie the prophecies of Orwell? The nation got a refreshing bath in the Bicentennial, rediscovering many old values. To set ourselves to make sure that 1984 the Book does not come true, but rather 1984, the Year of Enhancement, for individual and collective humanity—there is a target for tough minds.

DECEMBER 23
1966— On Greer Island we suddenly stumbled into an opening where three small children danced hilariously in a circle on top of a huge stump. If my mind had worked at all, I could have had their picture.

DECEMBER 24
1956— Christmas Eve in the city: I stood on lower Main Street for an hour waiting for a bus and saw among others sights: two drunks, one a scowling dark creature plainly seeking to shake off his companion, who was hatless and befuddled, trying to keep attached to his friend; two prostitutes, one a horrid shade of blond, with face rouged beyond belief, the other a squat black-haired Latino who gripped the blonde's arm as though to make sure she arrived at an assignation; an arthritic fellow who could only shuffle a few steps at a time;

a couple of Gypsy appearance; a man with a cane who bummed a quarter from me, assuring me he was really hungry, and he may have been. As I came nearer the center of town I thought I heard a man sobbing in some upstairs room.

DECEMBER 25

1977— Notwithstanding, I love a good book
full of wise sayings, or even not so wise.
It is like coming upon a chestful of gems
without having to sweat and groan with mud and clay
to obtain them. Still,
you can't really appreciate diamonds
unless you have worked in the mines.

DECEMBER 26

1969— A man should be able to feel
the graph of his going:
to know whether his trajectory is right,
to be able to say when in good time
he will reach his zenith.
Even though, like a burnt-out rocket,
he may not live to attainment.

DECEMBER 27

1977— When we came out into the night
a long white contrail stretched
across a quarter of the eastern sky,
ending just before it touched the full moon.
What enormous event had occurred
to raise such a vast exclamation point?

DECEMBER 28

1966— The faces on the street are leaves that fall at the on-set of winter. I can distinguish the type—the oak, the poplar, the cottonwood—but seldom does any individual form arrest attention. To fix upon a particular face is to enter into a life, a labyrinth. It may be done, likely enough, but only at the risk of pain or too short a delight.

DECEMBER 29

1980— Who would wish to be an unstruck match,
to lie in a state of chemical freeze,
a perfectly preserved combustion,
with no warmth or light?
For fear of becoming a smudged carbon,
would a true match give up
its one brief flare in the darkness?

DECEMBER 30

1974— Do not let the sun go down or the year disappear
without declaring the articles of love.

DECEMBER 31

1969— Children, I will tell you another story.
Men are animals. The God you desire to believe in
is a shadow. Love between Man and Woman
is also animal. Men have created fiction
because history is unbearable.
Virtue, like Sin, is relative;
at the worst it can be extenuated.
The exact measurements of Science
contain little rotten flaws.
Even Chance is not certain: it wavers
between altering and not altering.

Despite all these false quibbles
and sleazy pronouncements, if you will listen
to the rich evidence your own years will bring,
I greet you at the door
of your maturity.